D1503256

# AND YOU SHALL BE
# A BLESSING

# AND YOU SHALL BE A BLESSING

---

## An Unfolding of the Six Words That Begin Every *Brakhah*

Joel Lurie Grishaver

**JASON ARONSON INC.**
*Northvale, New Jersey*
*London*

This book was set in Palacio by Lind Graphics of Upper Saddle River, New Jersey, and printed at Haddon Craftsmen, in Scranton, Pennsylvania.

**Library of Congress Cataloging-in Publications Data**

Grishaver, Joel Lurie.
    And you shall be a blessing : an unfolding of the six words that
begin every brakhah / by Joel Laurie [sic] Grishaver.
        p.  cm.
    Includes index.
    ISBN 0-87668-464-9
    1. Benedictions—Sources.   2. Barukh atah Adonai Elohenu Melekh ha
-olam (The Hebrew phrase)  3. Judaism—Liturgy—Texts—History and
criticism.   4. Rabbinical literature—History and criticism.
    I. Title.
BM675.B4Z748  1993
296.7'2—dc20                                              92-28681

Manufactured in the United States of America. Jason Aronson Inc. offers books and cassettes. For information and catalog write to Jason Aronson Inc., 230 Livingston Street, Northvale, New Jersey 07647.

*For Alan and Jane, my partners, who both give my life context*
*and provide an ongoing defense.*
*They provide the place where this work can be done.*
*They are my real treasure.*

A faithful friend is a powerful defense.
One who has found such a friend has found a treasure.

Ben Sira 6:14

# Contents

vii

# Preface

This book began as far too much research for a children's textbook on one-line *brakhot*. My business partners are very good at allowing me the time to do academic writing and research, even if it does produce far too much information for any group of ten-year-olds. So, when *Basic Brakhot* became a book, this research took on a life of its own.

I teach regularly at the Department of Continuing Education at the University of Judaism. Soon this material found its way into some of my Talmud With Training Wheels class and then evolved into a semester on its own. In a class called "Making Sense of the Siddur," this material was first developed as a "stand-up" act, and then later read to my class. My students there literally drew this material out of me, and forced me to clarify it.

I then wrote it up and wondered. Two friends, Larry Kushner and Arthur Kurzweil, were kind enough to read and validate the manuscript. Arthur then offered me the chance to release it through Jason Aronson. (I had intended a longer and more obscure path.) When Arthur smiles on you, you feel good. He brought this manuscript out of the cold and toward fruition.

To all the parties who shaped, and taught, and helped: thank you.

Joel Lurie Grishaver

# Introduction

## I Learned to Pray on the School Yard—
## I Learned to Bless at the Dining Room Table

One Friday evening long ago, my sister Judy and I knocked a crystal dish filled with celery, pickles, and two kinds of olives off the dining room table and shattered it. I don't remember the exact time, but it was when we still lived on Babcock Street. Judy must have been in the six- to eight-year-old range—but, whatever her age—I was (and still am) four years older. I do remember that Judy and I were in the midst of a fight over who was going to pull the cover off the *hallah* and who would get to say *ha-Motzi*. The rules had long been clearly established—Judy lit the candles with my mother (usually with my father reminding my mother to always light the far candle first— something that took her years to master).[1] Then, I would lead

---

[1]For my father, this was a question of safety, not a religious practice. My mother sat at a corner of our table and the candles were

the family in *Kiddush*. Finally, the *hallah* and its *ha-Motzi* were something that we were supposed to alternate and rotate—one of us pulled the cover off while the other said the words. I don't even remember which was the more desirable half, the cover-pulling or the *brakhah*-saying, though I suspect that despite traditional Jewish priorities, pulling the cover off was probably what we considered the more compelling choice.

It is interesting to find in some long-abandoned corner of my memory a recollection that so closely echoes the biblical ideal that *brakhot* are worth fighting over. It is strange, or perhaps wonderfully appropriate, that now as I am finishing this book on the process of blessing (through writing its introduction), the real meaning of that Shabbat evening in the Babcock Street dining room comes as a way of explaining everything I have been trying to understand and say for over a year now—that *brakhot* are worth fighting over.

I learned how to pray on the baseball and football fields, on long walks home from school past the "bullies' corner," before exams, everywhere I didn't want something to happen. Standing in right field (in my own "field of nightmares"), hoping for the end of gym, the thought, "Dear God, please don't let the ball come anywhere near me and if it does come, don't let me drop it and make a fool out of myself," was among my most frequent religious expressions. Prayer was a way of hoping. It was an attempt to change the natural order.

*Brakhot* were done in the dining room. Six nights a week we ate in the kitchen without any kind of religious ceremony. But on The Seventh Night, the white table cloth was spread and we rested from all our labors with china, cloth napkins, a crystal tray with two kinds of olives, celery, and pickles, and with the saying of *brakhot*.

*Brakhot* were something we grew into. As far as I know, my parents said *brakhot* weekly long before I was born, but my

---

in the middle. To light the "far" candles second, my mother would have to reach past the lit "close candle."

sister and I had to grow into our roles as *brakhah*-sayers. First we watched, then we said them with our parents, and then finally we achieved independence. When we were around seven or eight and could say them perfectly, we entered the age of responsibility and became "candle-lighters," "*Kiddush*-makers," and "*ha-Motzi*-sayers." I still can remember the emotional pride of my first *Kiddush* solo—even though the details of the event are now faint.

In first and second grade in Sunday school, my teachers passed out these three-by-five cards with *brakhot* written in transliteration and translation. (Real Hebrew would come later.) We were supposed to memorize one a week. In those days, they took the curriculum one *brakhah* at a time, as if each was a significant skill and accomplishment. Today, the basic ritual formulae of Jewish life are embedded in my autopilot; I can mumble them as involuntary reflexes. Saying "candles," "*Kiddush*," and "*Motzi*" (as we called them) is now like breathing or having a pulse—an inplanted part of who I am, even when I choose not to dwell on them. But, once they were accomplishments: three-by-five cards that were studied, practiced, and performed, and transformed into a constellation of gold stars on a wall chart.

For me, prayer was a system of defenses against things I didn't want to happen. For example, "Dear God, I promise I will never hit my sister again if You let me get a B or better on tomorrow's spelling test" was really a positive way of saying, "Please don't let me fail." *Brakhah*-saying by contrast was a social ritual that brought everyday life into the dining room and therefore made it holy.

The Talmud has more or less the same vision of the distinction between prayer and *brakhah*; the rabbis saw it as a matter of tense. The discussion in question happens in the definition of the rituals of the Passover *seder* (*Pesahim* 116a ff.). It emerges as a tangent in a conversation about the role of the *Hallel* (acollection of psalms of praise that are said during the *seder* and other ocassions). A portion of the *Hallel* is said before the meal, and the rest is said after the meal.

### Mishnah (Pesahim 10:6)

How [much of the *Hallel*] should one recite [before eating]?:

The
School of
Shammai: Up to [the end of Psalm 113]: "As a joyous mother of children."

The
School of
Hillel: Up to [the end of Psalm 114:] "The flint into a fountain of water."

Then [the person] "seals" [the recitation with a *brakhah* of] redemption."

Rabbi
Tarphon: [Because they did not stipulate a specific *brakhah* formula] for this "seal," we need to indicate one. This *brakhah* should open:] "The One-Who-**Redeemed** Us and **Redeemed** our ancestors from Egpyt."

Rabbi
Akiva: [It should close] . . . "Blessed are You, *Adonai*, The One-Who-Has-**Redeemed** Israel."

### Gemara (Pesahim 117b)

[When the Babylonian rabbis were studying this passage, Raba asked a question about the wording of the closing formula of the *Hallel brakhah*.]

Raba: [The last prayer in the] *Shema* [and its *brakhot* (the *Ge'ulah*) and the *brakhah*] after the *Hallel* both end with "The One-Who-Has-**Redeemed** Israel," [which is in the past tense].

> The [fifth *brakhah* in the] *Amidah* [is on the same theme, but it is in the present tense]: The One-Who-**Redeems** Israel.
>
> A Voice:   [Why is there a difference?]
>
> Rabbi
> Zera:      The first two are [pure] *brakhot*; the last one is a [prayer of] petition.

The principle here indeed contrasts dining room and playground. *Brakhot* are dining room truths. They are the verification and recognition of the things that God has done. Saying *brakhot* is very much like talking about the news—commenting on things that have happened and are happening. Prayers are playground aspirations about what we hope will come to be—or hope will not come to be. They are attempts to change the world.

The distinction seems simple: A prayer = the expression "I want/need . . ."; A *brakhah* = the expression "You are great because . . ." However (as with most rabbinic lessons), the truth is not that simple and absolute. The fifth prayer in the *Amidah*, the one that Rabbi Zera contends is a "prayer of petition" is actually a *"brakhah* of petition"—it is sealed with the words *"Barukh Atah Adonai . . ."* This is not a contradiction; rather, it reveals a complexity of thinking.

To explain: the middle *brakhot* in the *Amidah* are indeed very direct statements of petition. They are a spiritual shopping list, made up of the things we feel we need from God—now. They are statements of dependency, acknowledgments of our weaknesses and our limitations, and therefore expressions of faith. In every act of asking God—petitioning—there is an element of praise, a statement of God's potential to make a difference. Without that potential—without the acknowledgment of God as the source of blessing—the petition makes no sense. In making a petition we both admit our own dependency on forces beyond ourselves, and in directing our petitions to God, we are affirming our belief in God's ability to help us. In a sense, every petition is a hidden statement of praise. We are acknowledging the importance of the Entity asked for help.

Likewise, every act of praise disguises a petition. When we compliment a child or a parent or a friend or even an enemy, for having done something extraordinary, we are entreating them to repeat the action. Every statement of praise contains a secret petition: "Please do that again." Therefore, in praising God for food or rainbows, health or the redemption of the Jewish people, we are simultaneously saying, "Please do that again."

The *Hallel* and the last blessing in the *Shema* cycle, the *brakhot* that end: "The One-Who-Has-**Redeemed** Israel," are historical reflections. In praising God, these prayers bring us back to Egypt, have us stand on the banks of the Red Sea, have us struggle on the very brink of existence—and then firsthand, through historical spiritual reflection—have us reexperience a redemption. The message, one rooted firmly in biblical thinking, is that our past guarantees our future. In saying that God has **redeemed** Israel, we are also expressing faith in (and in a sense a petitioning of) the final and complete **redemption**. In his seminal commentary, *The Weekday Siddur*, B. S. Jacobson explains:

> Set within the framework of this *brakhah*, the above-mentioned verse (Jeremiah 31:10), "For *Adonai* saved Jacob and redeemed him from a hand that was stronger than his own," is included as added evidence that God redeemed the people of Israel in the past from the powerful Egyptian nation. Yet, when we examine the prophecy as a whole that constitutes the *Haftarah* for the second day of *Rosh ha-Shanah*, it becomes clear that the subject under discussion is the redemption of the future, and the very verbs "redeemed" and "delivered" are worded in the *prophetic past* [emphasis added], i.e., they speak of the future, as if it had already become the past. Since God will certainly fulfill His promise in the future, it is possible to speak as if the events have already occurred.[2]

---

[2]B. S. Jacobson, *The Weekday Siddur: An Exposition and Analysis of its Structure, Contents, Language and Ideas* (Tel Aviv: "Sinai" Publishing, 1978), p. 230.

Therefore, every act of praising something God has already done (a *brakhah*) is both an expression of gratitude for what God has done and a petition of hope that our faith in the ultimate reception of a full-benefits package will be actualized. Every blessing is both a statement of belief and an expression of hope in the once and future *brakhah*—the final blessing.

Present-tense petitions are emergency calls. They do not deny that God will ultimately redeem and save and free and feed, and so on. They don't reject or abandon redemption on a prophetic scale. Instead, *brakhot* of petition simply say, "Now, please—today, if possible." They take place in the pressure of the playground, not the reflection of the dining room. But, as we have seen, the two moments are not detached—they are not separate forms of human communication with the Divine. Rather, they are simply opposite ends of a continuum that runs from past experience to present need. They simply operate on different levels of desperation.

This book is designed to look at six words, familiar words, "table" words. Its purpose is to finally unfold the full power of words memorized from three-by-five cards that once earned gold stars on a Hebrew school wall chart and are now regularly mumbled at communal Jewish gatherings. This book looks to make the mumbling of such prayers as intense and emotionally driven as were the prayers of this former ten-year-old who was sincerely afraid—afraid with all his being—that a ball would come his way in deep right field, that he would drop it, or that his throw would never reach the infield, and that any social future he might ever have would instantly be over.

By consulting with rabbinic sources, we learn that the "past" is in some ways the "future" and that the present is a demand for a future that comes sooner. These tenses, once understood, influence our understanding of prayer. This simple issue of tenses is but the first step of the journey we must take. The unfolding of the *brakhah* formula requires that we go on a circuitous journey of association—a spiritual pilgrimage through books and literature ancient and modern—because the secret to rubbing these six *brakhah*-starting words and having them work their magic is not just found in their pure meaning but rather in their associations. Each of these words is bonded to important ideas and discussions. They recall important historical moments and small, subtle insights. When we've made these grand rounds (one of many such possible explorations), a great new whole formed of these six small parts should be readily visible.

When my sister Judy and I fought over the right to perform the *hallah* rite, we were re-creating the biblical struggles between Jacob and Esau, both of whom also fought over blessings. While they fought over receiving a blessing and we fought over making a *brakhah*, the fights were really one and the same. As we unfold the words of the *brakhah* formula, we will learn that "saying" a *brakhah* is the first step in "becoming" a blessing—and that being a blessing is indeed receiving all the gifts we are seeking. *Brakhot* are indeed worth fighting for—because *brakhot* actually are accomplishments.

# 1

# Anything You Say—Can and Will

The *brakhah* formula is made up of four basic elements: the *Barukh*, the *Shem*, the *Malkhut*, and the *Mitzvah* insertion.

The *brakhah* formula acts as an access code.

> You have the right to remain silent.
> Anything you say, can and will be used against you in a court of law.
> You have the right to have an attorney present.
> If you cannot afford an attorney, one will be provided for you.
> Do you understand these rights?

These are words we know very well. They have become part of our cultural backdrop. Law enforcement officers say these words because of a person by the name of Miranda, who was found innocent (even though he was probably guilty)—the Supreme Court of the United States decided that any person has the right to be aware of his or her rights. Rather than leave the matter to chance, police departments (informed by their

1

district attorney's offices) choose to have their officers deliver this statement of rights precisely in a manner that is clearly legally binding.

Police officers "read" criminals their rights rather than "telling" them (in a personal way) or expressing them spontaneously and creatively, because it assures the probability of a conviction. Not to do so opens up the *possibility* of error. Legal formulas achieve that end. Legal formulas such as "The whole truth and nothing but the truth," "I pledge allegiance," "In Sickness and in Health," "By the powers invested in me," insure the precise transmission of a message. (Nothing can assure its reception.)

In Jewish communal worship, the prayers found in the *siddur* (prayer book) are built out of fixed, legal formulae. The basic building block of Jewish prayer is a format called a *brakhah*, a blessing or a benediction. To be a *brakhah*, a prayer must use one of three precisely defined variations of a formula beginning with the words: בָּרוּךְ אַתָּה יהוה.

## Brakhot

For the rabbis, the architects (or perhaps better, interior designers) of the Jewish tradition, it was important that every *brakhah* tell "the truth," the precise truth—because it is critical to be truthful and exact when we are speaking of God. Just as the district attorney wants to be sure that no half-truth or confusion drifts into the suspects' perceptions of their rights, so too, the rabbis wanted to make sure that no statement of blessing would confuse or distort the truth about God, the Source-of-All-Blessings. Therefore, they built the Jewish worship experience around a series of "legal" religious formulae, statements of truth, called *brakhot*.

**The Teaser**

Look at this number:

**16175663451**

It tells a whole story. Can you retell it? It is hiding a number of secrets. Do you know them? It holds a universe of meanings.

Do you understand them? What does this number say to you? What does it mean? And if it is not obvious, how do you go about unlocking its meaning?

Try commas. You can divide it into hundreds, thousands, and millions, but that will get you nowhere. You can take out your calculator and look for mysterious factors or perfect squares or multiples of pi, but to the best of my knowledge, that will lead you nowhere. Likewise, you can try to find meaning in the number of times 1, 3, 4, 5, 6, and 7 are used, or speculate on why the 2 is missing, but this too is a dead-end. So is any attempt to find historical significance to the dates 1617, 1756, and so on. If you add all the numbers together, you'll come up with 45. It is a nice number, but it is not a story, a secret, or a meaning.

## The Secret Pattern

The real secret is hyphens. If you put them in the right places, everything is revealed: 1-617-566-3451. Even though the information was there before, now that you see the pattern, you understand almost everything. Think about it.

The "1" is the first clue. It says, "This is a long-distance call." In most cities, you have to dial a "1" before you make a long-distance call. The "1" works like a switch. When the computer hears the tone for the one (or counts one click if it is an old-fashioned rotary dial), it shunts the call out of the local circuits and into the long-distance track.

There are, however, other clues to the same lesson. In some cities, you don't have to dial the "1." Instead, the phone computers use another clue to direct a long distance call. The 617 is an "area" code. You can tell that both from the position and from the 1 in the middle. All area codes (and no prefixes) have either 1 or 0 in the middle. That's another way the call is tracked as long distance. In this case, 617 is the eastern part of Massachusetts. The computer hears the three numbers of the "area" code and directs the call to somewhere near Boston. Now that some of the secrets have been unlocked, let's look for the story.

The 566 is the "prefix." It is the first of seven digits that make up the home phone number. In fact, this phone number is the home phone number of my boyhood. In those days, 566 was **LO**ngwood **6**. It was one of three "prefixes" used in Brookline. We also had **AS**penwal **7** and **RE**gent **4** (734 originally went to South Brookline, the expensive part of town). When the computer hears 566, it switches the call into the "Brookline circuits" and into the 566 bank of numbers.

The 3451 was the personal identification number of my home telephone. Many phones in the country had 3451 as their final numbers, but only one 566 number in area code 617 could end that way.

**Access Codes**

In computer speak, a phone number is really an access code. Its formula guides the message along a particular path to a specific destination. Think of it as a huge railroad yard, each cluster of numbers representing a switching point and each number telling the switcher which path to follow.

## *Brakhot*: A Definition

The *brakhah* is the basic building block of Jewish prayer. *Brakhot* are said as individual experiences occur, and chains of *brakhot* form the backbone of Jewish communal worship. A *brakhah* is a prayer that uses a formula:

בָּרוּךְ אַתָּה יהוה אֱלֹהֵינוּ מֶלֶךְ הָעוֹלָם
*Barukh Atah Adonai Eloheinu Melekh ha-Olam*

Praised are You *Adonai*, Our God, The Ruler-of-the-Cosmos.

Some *brakhot* insert an additional formula:

אֲשֶׁר קִדְּשָׁנוּ בְּמִצְוֹתָיו וְצִוָּנוּ
*asher kidshanu b'mitzvotav, v'tzivanu . . .*

The One-Who-Makes-Us-Holy with (His) the *mitzvot*, and made it a *mitzvah* for us. . . .

Only *mitzvah-brakhot* use this addition. In fact, it is this addition that "switches" the *brakhah* onto the *mitzvah* track.

If you've known these words since you were young, you've memorized them, recited them, forgotten them, relearned them, mumbled them, didn't recite them, and then again did recite them a whole number of times. Probably, though, they were a black box, a meaningless jumble like 16172443444. In this book we're going to put in the hyphens and unlock the pattern. We will examine each of the connections made by this rabbinic access code and thereby be able to trace some of the paths to Jewish prayer. We will look for spiritual hyphens that give meaning to the jumble of syllables.

## The Anatomy of a *Brakhah*

The *brakhah* formula has three distinct parts: The *Barukh*, the *Shem*, and the *Malkhut*. Each of these parts has a different function. Each part makes a different spiritual "connection." (That it is how the formula acts as an access code.)

1. The *Barukh*                                                         בָּרוּךְ

Every *brakhah* uses the word *Barukh*. Without it, a prayer is a prayer, not a *brakhah*. *Barukh* is the definitional element in a blessing.

*Barukh* is the process—the action. It defines the process. While we will speak of "*barukh*-ing" in Chapters Three and Four, it is enough to say here that saying a *brakhah* is the creation of a certain kind of mental and spiritual focus—a process of radical awareness, learning, growth, and change—and the opening word, the *barukh*, establishes the direction of this movement.

2. The *Shem*                                                     אַתָּה יהוה

To be a "kosher" *brakhah* (kosher = acceptable for Jewish use), a *brakhah* must also contain the words: *Atah Adonai*. This portion of the *brakhah* formula is called the *Shem*.

*Shem* means "name." *Adonai* is God's name. (It is like Fred or Barbara.) It is a form of direct address. But it also implies more. It also recalls a specific, intimate relationship. In Chapter 6 of Exodus, God speaks to Moses:

I am יהוה (*Adonai*).
I appeared to Abraham, Isaac, and Jacob as *El Shaddai*
[God from On High],
But I did not make Myself known by My Name יהוה *Adonai*
I also established My covenant with them
to give them the land of Canaan . . .

We learn from this passage that *Adonai* (the place holder for the Tetragrammaton—the four-letter nonpronouncable name of God) is a private name, a family name if you will, uniquely available to the Jewish people. *Adonai* is the God of Jewish history, the God of the covenant, the God of the special relationship between God and Israel. When we call God *Adonai*, we are using "the private line," one not generally available to the rest of humanity.

3. *Malkhut*                                    אֱלֹהֵינוּ מֶלֶךְ הָעוֹלָם

Every *brakhah* must also contain (or be connected to[1] the phrase *Eloheinu Melekh ha-Olam*. This describes God as *Melekh* (Ruler) and is called *Malkhut*.

*Malkhut* means Rulership.[2] It is a job description. Likewise,

---

[1]*Brakhot* can be strung together to form *brakhah*-chains. In these *brakhah* chains, only the first *brakhah* in the series needs to have *Malkhut* mentioned; the rest can use only *Barukh Atah Adonai*.

[2]*Malkhut* is a masculine term. In most settings you will find it translated as "Kingship." My choice of "Rulership" is ideological and, I believe, merits some explanation. I have a few women friends who have shared with me their hurt at always feeling left out of a religion made for "him" and having to relate to the God "He." The Jewish tradition evolved through periods of time when males dominated the leadership and did most of the writing. There was a tendency (as was

*Eloheinu* (Our God) is also a job description. God is a role (fulfilled by *Adonai*).

But, while defining *Adonai*'s role as Ruler and God, we are also recalling a second relationship. *Adonai* is Ruler-of-All-People, Creator-of-the-Whole-Cosmos, God-of-All. *Malkhut* is universal; it is the God experience available to any person who looks at the world, experiences creation, reflects on truth, and seeks the spiritual. While *Adonai* is the God of Jewish history, *Melekh ha-Olam* is the God experience available to all.

4. The *Mitzvah* Insertion　　　　. . . אֲשֶׁר קִדְּשָׁנוּ בְּמִצְוֹתָיו וְצִוָּנוּ

As we have said earlier, this insertion changes the *brakhah* from a "pleasure *brakhah*"—a response to one of the wonders of God's creation—to a *"mitzvah brakhah"*—the anticipation of a new, prescribed religious experience.

1-617-566-3451, Amen.

---

culturally consistent then) to use the pronoun "he" to talk about a Jew and to use masculine language when talking about God. *Shekhinah*, the name given to the "In-Dwelling-Presence" (the neighborly aspect of God), is one of many notable exceptions where feminine God-language was the intentional choice of the rabbis. In the educational materials I produce, I have always chosen to be sensitive to my friends' feelings. My translations are carefully reworked to reflect a nongender-specific understanding of the Jewish tradition. Similar care is taken with passages I create. In working with material from the *siddur*, however, I sometimes break this self-imposed commitment. While my original writing still strives to include carefully chosen pronouns and images of the Jew "she" as well as the Jew "he," my translations of liturgy often reflect the Hebraic use of the masculine form. This inconsistency (which you will also find in this volume) is a compromise, reflecting a commitment to Hebrew mastery. In the case of the *siddur*, students often compare the translation against the original text, as a way of extrapolating meaning. For this particular function, that I view as a very important step in learning how to pray with a Hebrew text, a nongender-specific reworking creates far too much confusion. Therefore, I've balanced two different ideological commitments. While a male-dominated expression of the Jewish tradition is part of Jewish history, it need not be part of the Jewish future.

# 2

# Preprogrammed Spontaneous Gratification

**The rabbis who wrote our prayers insisted on using a formula because they believed that a "fixed" liturgy is the best path to sincere spiritual "spontaneity."**

### Benjamin's Sandwich: A Case Study

Here is the problem:

Benjamin the Shepherd made a sandwich and said in his "first" language (Aramaic, not Hebrew), "Blessed be the Master of this bread."

Benjamin said this spontaneous *brakhah* with real feeling. He really was grateful for the sandwich he was about to eat and his intention in saying this prayer was to sincerely thank the One God for the special blessing of having bread to eat.

Benjamin did not say:

9

בָּרוּךְ אַתָּה יהוה הַזָּן אֶת הַכֹּל
*Barukh Atah Adonai Hazan et ha-Kol*

Was this spontaneous celebration of God's creation (etc.) an acceptable *brakhah*?

In the Talmud, *Brakhot* 40b, the rabbis argue over this particular case. In their debate we are able to uncover some of their reasons why the *brakhah* formula was created. To understand some of the dynamics of the *brakhah* formula, we are going to work our way through that discussion.

### The Origin of *Brakhot* (A General History)

*Brakhot* are human creations (though some traditional sources attribute their origins to the angels). They are the product of the rabbinic imagination—the rabbis' creative extension of principles and insights found in the Torah.

Now it's time to "**Meet the Rabbis.**"

Around 30 B.C.E. the end of Jewish life (as it had been known) was occurring.

Augustus had defeated Mark Anthony (think Cleopatra), and King Herod was granted power in *Eretz Yisrael* (The Land of Israel). In quick succession, the revolts and protests began (think of all of those Christian costumed epics). In 66 C.E. the Great Revolt started—Jerusalem is besieged. By 70 C.E., it falls and the Temple is destroyed. By 73 C.E. Masada has fallen, too. Life is pretty depressing.

But, meanwhile, Yohanan ben Zakkai has set up shop (or more specifically, "school") in Yavneh and the rabbinic process gets down to serious work. In 114 C.E., encouraged by Rabbi Akiva (the leading rabbinical type of his era), the last major revolt against the Romans, the Bar Kokhba War, begins. In 117 C.E. Bar Kokhba is defeated. Most of the remaining rabbinical leadership was killed in the process. Now, the end is in sight.

By 200 c.e., Jewish life in what is now "Palestina" is no longer viable. While a few Jews remain, the center of Jewish life has become Babylonia.

One of the major centers of Jewish life is located there, within the "Ivy League" *yeshivot*, the rabbinical academies. Here, Jewish life remains vibrant, until about 500 c.e.

This five-hundred-and-fifty-year period represents a dynamic transition. During it, Judaism transformed itself from a political nationality to a blend of ethnicity, culture, and religion. And this new religious identity has transformed itself from a national-religious cult, centered in the Temple, to a family/community-home/synagogue "portable" way of life. The chief designers, engineers, crisis counselors, and instigators of this transformation are the group of Pharisaic scholars we call "the rabbis." It is not the purpose of this book to tell their story in great detail; but we cannot really unlock the meaning of the *siddur*, one of their many classic best-sellers (including the *Mahzor*, the *Haggadah*, the *Mishnah*, the Talmud, and the *Midrash*) without involving ourselves with them.

## *Mishnah* + *Gemara* = Talmud

The Talmud, the quintessential document of rabbinic thinking, is divided into two layers. The first is called *Mishnah*. The *Mishnah* is a law code, written between 30 b.c.e. and 200 c.e. in *Eretz Yisrael*. Essentially, the *Mishnah* is a set of conclusions. It reads like a municipal law code, telling people what to do, but for the most part masking the reasoning behind those laws. Consider this analogy:

**Layer One:** A city passes a law setting a $25 fee for crossing a nonresidential street in the wrong way (jay walking). The law carefully talks about intersections, crosswalks, and lights. It tells the police and the judges just who should receive a ticket.

The law does not contain a rationale for the law. It does not explain that the jay-walking laws were designed to save lives. All of those issues, the reasoning and the debate, took place in the city council (and might be part of their records) but didn't need to be part of the actual ordinance.

**Layer Two:** Twenty years later, a test case is brought to a court. A police officer cites a person for jay walking at 4 A.M. The person refuses to pay, arguing, "That the intent of the law was public safety, and at 4 A.M., there is no question of public safety." In the court room, there is a need to reconstruct the "intent" of the law, and decide if the 4 A.M. case should change the enforcement of the jay-walking statute.

This second half of this process, this questioning of intent and application, parallels the *Gemara*. Years later, a new generation of rabbis was forced to reapply old laws to new conditions. To do so, they needed to reconstruct the reasoning behind the *Mishnah* and decide its relevancy to a new situation. The *Gemara*, this second layer, was written between 200 and 500 C.E. in Babylonia.[1]

## Learning about *Brakhah* Formula from the Talmud

### A Practice *Mishnah*

The first book of the Talmud is called *Brakhot*. From it we can trace the story of the creation of Jewish communal worship. It includes transcripts of the very discussions where the forms of Jewish worship we use today were invented and extrapolated. As we study the tractate *Brakhot*, we can watch the transformation of Jewish worship from a national sacrificial cult to a daily book-centered communal experience.

In the sixth chapter of *Mishnah Brakhot* we find a series of

---

[1]A second *Gemara*, the Jerusalem Talmud, was created in parallel in *Eretz Yisrael*, but for our purposes it is not significant. It exists, not so much as a document that is studied independently, but only compared at points of interest. While there are technically two Talmuds, when Jews speak of the Talmud, they are talking about the Babylonian Talmud.

laws about when *brakhot* should be said. (Think of our Traffic Rule—all about practice with no statement of purpose.) The chapter begins with this *Mishnah*. This *Mishnah*, *Brakhot* 6:1, is a good "practice" *Mishnah* that will allow us to learn how to read this material and will teach us an important lesson.

**a.**

What *brakhot* are said over fruit?

Over the fruit of the tree one says:
בּוֹרֵא פְּרִי הָעֵץ *Borai P'ri ha-Etz*
(The One-Who-Creates the fruit of the tree)

—Except for wine, over which one says:
בּוֹרֵא פְּרִי הַגָּפֶן *Borai P'ri ha-Gafen*
(The One-Who-Creates the fruit of the vine).

Our *Mishnah* begins, as many do, with a rhetorical question. We can learn from this question that this *Mishnah* will be a list of which *brakhot* "are said over" which fruit. The first "answer" found in the first section is simple: (Almost all) "tree-fruit" get a "tree-fruit" *brakhah*. The exception is wine, which gets a "vine-fruit" *brakhah*. The unstated question that is posed but not answered is, "Why is wine an exception?" (For the purposes of rabbinic biology, a "vine" could have been considered to be a tree—it does have a trunk, roots, leaves, and branches.)

**b.**

Over things that grow in the ground one says:
בּוֹרֵא פְּרִי הָאֲדָמָה *Borai P'ri ha-Adamah*
(The One-Who-Creates the fruit of the ground)

—Except for bread, over which one says:
הַמּוֹצִיא לֶחֶם מִן הָאָרֶץ *ha-Motzi Lehem min ha-Aretz*
(The One-Who-Brings-Forth bread from the earth).

The second part of the *Mishnah* is a carbon copy of structure of
the the first. "Tree-fruit" all trigger one *brakhah*, with one
exception: wine. "Ground-fruit" all trigger one *brakhah* (a
different *brakhah*) with one exception: bread. Again, we are left
to wonder about the reason for that exception. A pattern is
developing.

c.

Over vegetables one says:
בּוֹרֵא פְּרִי הָאֲדָמָה *Borai P'ri ha-Adamah*
(The One-Who-Creates the fruit of the ground)

—But Rabbi Judah said: One says:
בּוֹרֵא מִינֵי דְשָׁאִים *Borai M'nai De-shaim*
(The One-Who-Creates all kinds of herbs).

Part "c" (our label, not a traditional label) breaks the pattern. It
does not teach a general rule and an exception. Now, in the
third section we have an argument. "Vegetables" create a
problem. There are two opinions: the unnamed opinion (the
majority) think that they are another form of "ground-fruit,"
while Rabbi Judah believes that they should be considered a
new category, "Herbs." Part "c" is essentially a clarification of
part "b"; we are clarifying the parameters of "ground-fruit."

This passage is a very typical *mishnah* (in Jewish English we
call a "piece" of the *Mishnah*, "a *mishnah*"). Look at it and you
will see that while the rules are clearly given, the reasons for
those rules are not even suggested. Even the disputed blessing
(Rabbi Judah's versus the majority) contains no explanation.

Were we to study this *mishnah* in detail, we would have two
tasks. First, we would review the rules that were taught. Then,
we would seek the core of the *mishnah*, struggling to break out
the logic and the meaning of each of these *brakhot*. We would
struggle to find out why these specific *brakhot* were created and
what they were supposed to accomplish. While we could reach
some of this through Holmes-like "deductive reasoning," it is
often easier to just turn to the *Gemara*. To fully understand this

*mishnah*, we need its *gemara*—it is there that purpose becomes a major issue.

To ease frustration, let's (for the sake of information) share those explanations:

a. "Tree-Fruit" is one category of food.

Wine is an exception and receives a different *brakhah* because it serves a ritual role as the substance over which the *Kiddush* is normatively said.

b. "Ground-Fruit" is a second category of food.

Bread is an exception, because as "the staff of life," it serves as the definitional element at a meal. (In simple language, the *brakhah ha-Motzi* over bread covers all food eaten at a meal).

c. Rabbi Judah believes that there are three kinds of food that grow in the ground: "ground-fruit" such as strawberries, whose fruit we eat; "pulse" (like peas), whose seeds we eat; and "greens" (like lettuce, asparagus, etc.), where we eat the leaves. He thinks that each category should have its own *brakhah*, but the majority overrules him (he's gotten obsessively too specific).

The important lesson taught by this *mishnah* (it's caramel-coated center) is that both patterns and exceptions have meaning. Each kind of food should have its own *brakhah* (but don't totally obsess over it) and foods that have a special ritual role should be made special with a unique *brakhah*.

In other words, it is good for us to have a unique moment of contemplation over each thing we eat, acknowledging God's involvement in the unique food item we are about to consume. In doing so, we grow in our appreciation of the diverse and distinct facets of God's creation. Eating can be a "nature" lesson (if we have to say *brakhot*), and those *brakhot* in turn make the nature lesson into a spiritual experience—eating.

## Our *Mishnah*—The One that Triggers the Argument over Benjamin's Sandwich

The second *mishnah* of this chapter reveals a little bit of the logic behind these *brakhot*. It shows us that each *brakhah* must be "factual." Again, it is done in the form of "rules," not "explanations." It goes like this:

If a person says:
בּוֹרֵא פְּרִי הָאֲדָמָה *Borai P'ri ha-Adamah*
(The One-Who-Created the fruit of the ground)
over a fruit that grows on a tree, the *mitzvah* has been fulfilled.

But if one says בּוֹרֵא פְּרִי הָעֵץ *Borai P'ri ha-Etz*
(The One-Who-Created the fruit of the tree)
over fruit that grew in the ground, the *mitzvah* has not been fulfilled.

In any case, if the person says
שֶׁהַכֹּל נִהְיֶה בִּדְבָרוֹ *she-ha-Kol Nihiyeh b'Dvar-o*
(That everything was created by His Word),
the *mitzvah* has been fulfilled.

The basic point of this *mishnah* is simple. *Brakhot* must make true statements. It is all right to say the "ground-fruit" *brakhah* over fruit that grows on a tree because the tree grows in the ground. It is a true statement. It is *not* all right to say a "tree-fruit" *brakhah* over fruit that grows in the ground, because it isn't true. *Brakhot*, which talk about God, have to tell the truth—otherwise they are false advertising.

The last part of this *brakhah* introduces the "omnibus *brakhah*," *she-ha-Kol*. It is designed as a way-out. When you aren't sure what the right *brakhah* is, *she-ha-Kol* covers you, because no matter what the food, the statement "That all was created by (God's) Word" is always true.

But this omnibus *brakhah* leaves a new unanswered question. That question is the *Gemara*'s starting point. It begins by asking; "What is the purpose of all the other *brakhot*? If *she-ha-Kol* will always do, why do we need to learn all of these other specific *brakhot*?"

## The Debate over Benjamin's Sandwich

We go now to the floor of some Babylonian Academy to join the debate (*Brakhot* 40b) in progress.

a.

Rabbi 1: [Would it be acceptable for a person to say the *brakhah*: *she-ha-Kol Nehiyeh b'Dvar-o* ("That everything exists because of His Word") over foods that have a specific *brakhah* assigned?

Narrator: [There are two opinions.] We have been taught that Rabbi Huna ruled:

Rabbi Huna: [*she-ha-Kol* is acceptable in every case] except bread and wine.

Narrator: While Rabbi Yohanan ruled:

Rabbi Yohanan: [*she-ha-Kol* is also acceptable] even for bread and wine.

[Narrator: Rashi, a famous medieval Jewish commentator, explains Rabbi Huna's position this way:

Rashi: Bread is an exception, because it is considered to be the essence of a meal. Wine is also a special case because it is connected to *Kiddush*, the perception of holiness. The *Gemara* explains these exceptions later in the discussion on page 42b.]

The discussion in the *Gemara* begins by asking if the omnibus food *brakhah*: *she-ha-Kol Nihiyeh b'Dvar-o* (a.k.a. *she-ha-Kol*) can really be used for all foods. In answering this question, the *Gemara* reveals that the rabbis of the *Mishnah*, the ones who wrote these rules (and created *brakhot*), didn't agree. One school said, "Bread and wine demand their own special *brakhot*." This echoes what we already learned in the first *Mishnah* in chapter 6 of *Brakhot*—wine and bread are exceptions. Another school said, "No problem; use it for any food." This echoes the *Mishnah* found that triggers this section, in which *brakhot* are acceptable (even though they might not be precise) as long as they are truthful. That is the message of a "ground-fruit" *brakhah* being acceptable for a "tree fruit."

The text of the *Gemara* doesn't resolve this debate, although you already know its resolution, because it is the Jewish practice we still follow. While *she-ha-Kol* might fulfill the technical requirements of "thanking God" and "being a true statement," it doesn't maximize the experience. The unique spiritual potentials of "bread" and "wine" are better fulfilled by unique *brakhot*. Having had the discussion, the matter is now closed. The technically acceptable formula (while theoretically a possible solution) is no longer a viable Jewish choice when a spiritual insight is waiting to be released. Just by remembering a few words (and not a single formula), a new insight into God's creation awaits us. That is why we always say *ha-Motzi* and *Birkat Ya'in* (the wine *brakhah*) and never employ (over wine and bread) *she-ha-Kol*. Acceptable, in this case, just isn't best.

### b.

Having reached this impass, the *Gemara* goes off on the tangent that interests us. They ask, "As long as we are debating the obligation to use a precise matching of *brakhot* to actions, how do we know that *brakhot* must use a precise formula?"

As we listen, it becomes clear that for the *Tannaim*, the rabbis of the *Mishnah*, *brakhot* were still evolving. They were a new "tool" whose applications were just being clearly delineated.

We are watching not just the creation of some basic religious policy, but the actual evolution of a spiritual process.

Narrator:     [It is clear that even the *Tannaim*, the rabbis of the *Mishnah*] didn't agree about the exact use of *brakhot*. After all,] we have been taught in a *baraita* [a source from the time of the *Mishnah* that was not included in the *Mishnah*, but is quoted here.]

Rabbi
Meir:        If a person sees a loaf of bread and says:

Person:      "What a fine loaf of bread this is! Bless *ha-Makom* [a name for God], Who Created it.

Rabbi
Meir:        This person has fulfilled the *mitzvah* . . . .

Rabbi
Yosi:        [I think you are wrong.] If a person changes the formula "minted" by the rabbis, that person has not fulfilled the obligation . . . .

Here, the talmudic discussion recalls an older argument between two *Tannaim*. Rabbi Meir and Rabbi Yosi argue over the case of a person who blesses bread with the right spirit, but with improvised words. Meir says that the improvised blessing is acceptable, while Yosi demands the precise rabbinic formula of *ha-Motzi* (or, as we will see later, of *Birkat ha-Mazon*—the after-eating *brakhah* cycle). The debate rages on.

c.

To resolve this argument between "form" and "intent," the *Gemara* then cites another old case.

Narrator:     [We find Rabbi Meir supported in a famous *baraita* about a ruling Rav made, "The Case of

Benjamin's Sandwich."] Benjamin, the shepherd, made a sandwich, [ate it,] and then said in Aramaic [the local language, which is not Hebrew].

Benjamin: Blessed be The Master-of-this-Bread.

Narrator: [Rav ruled:]

Rav: He has fulfilled his obligation to say a *brakhah* after eating.

Student: [No way! That can't be! Wrong! This *brakhah* doesn't mention God's name. Anyone could be the master of the bread. Benjamin could even be blessing himself. How could] Rav [accept this as a *brakhah*?] I thought he taught:

Rav: Any *brakhah* that doesn't mention God's name is not a real *brakhah*.

## d.

Narrator: Then we must guess that [we have remembered this event incorrectly. We must have recalled a wrong version of Benjamin's Aramaic *brakhah*. Because Rav accepted it (and to meet his requirement), Benjamin] must have said [something like]:

Benjamin: Blessed be The All-Merciful, The Master-of-this-Bread . . . .

This time the *Gemara* consults its memory and recalls a parallel case: Benjamin's Dagwood. Benjamin, too, said an improvised *brakhah*. However, in the case of Benjamin, they had a record that stated that Rav had justified the *brakhah*, even though it was spontaneous.

However, there is an objection. Rav's acceptance of this spontaneous *brakhah* seems to contradict another principle he had taught earlier, that the *Shem* part, the part that names *Adonai*, must be included in every *brakhah*. Rav's argument here is that to be acceptable, a *brakhah* must both express the right feelings and make it clear that *Adonai* (the One God) and not some other god, is the One being blessed. Therefore, Rav couldn't have accepted this spontaneous (nonnamed) *brakhah* of Benjamin. Something is wrong (the accurate preservation of teachings from *Mishnah* times must have broken down somewhere).

To solve this contradiction, the *Gemara* (in what we have called part "d") re-searches its memory banks and concludes that an alternate version of Benjamin's *brakhah*: Blessed be The All-Merciful, the Master of this bread . . . " must be the actual one which was said. This second version works because "The All-Merciful" is a rabbinic euphemism for God, making it clear that *Adonai* is the one being blessed. This time, even though Benjamin's spontaneous *brakhah* doesn't follow the wording of the rabbinic formula, it does define the One God as the source of *brakhot*.

Next (in a portion, "e," not cited here) the discussion continues, establishing that while Hebrew is preferable, a *brakhah* can be said in any language.

## f.[2]

Then the discussion of Rav's analysis leads us to another *baraita*. This *baraita* is another reexamination of Rav's *brakhah* rule.

Narrator:   Earlier, we mentioned [part of this *baraita*]:

Rav:        I think that any *brakhah* that does not mention *Shem* [God's name] is not a real *brakhah*.

Narrator:   Rabbi Yohanan disagreed.

---

[2]No, we didn't skip letters. These headings refer to sections of the full text of the *sugiah* (talmudic discussion), which is found in the source section of this book.

Rabbi
Yohanan:   Any *brakhah* that doesn't mention [both *Shem*
           and *Malkhut* (God being the ruler)] isn't a real
           *brakhah*.

The actual *sugiah* (conversation) goes on for another couple
of sentences. In it, the rabbis establish the biblical roots of both
Rav's and Rabbi Yohanan's arguments. It the end, Rabbi
Yohanan wins. This echoes the position taken earlier in the
discussion by Rabbi Yosi, "If a person changes the formula
'minted' by the rabbis, that person has not fulfilled the obligation. . . ." While the rabbis understand that Benjamin's *brakhah*
(and others like it) may be valid religious expressions well
within the Jewish tradition, they prefer Jews to use a precise
formula in response to precise events.

## Legal Formulae

As we suggested at the opening of this book, this is analo-
gous to the American legal system, where a police officer
"reads" a criminal her rights rather than "telling" them (in a
personal way); the Jew who prays with a formula has used the
legal language that precisely expresses the truth. This notion of
using the precise truth when speaking of God is precisely the
message we learned from *Brakhot* 6:2, the *Mishnah* that explained that it was all right to say the "ground-fruit" *brakhah*
over tree fruit, but not *vice versa*.

Thus we can conclude from this talmudic passage:

a. Even though we can say a *brakhah* in any language, it is still
   preferable to say it in Hebrew.[3]

---

[3] This question of Hebrew language is discussed in this *sugiah* but
not in the parts we have cited in this section. It can, however, be
found in the full version of this text, which is included in the
Appendix.

b. Even if a spontaneous, well-meant *brakhah* may be acceptable, it is still better to follow the "minted" formula.

I hope by now you are thinking about the word "minted." I wanted it to catch your attention. In the next chapter its purpose will be made clear.

## How the Rabbis Fixed the *Brakhah*'s Formula: An Explanation

A clue about rabbinic thought: If you ask a talmudic-type rabbi, "Which is better, A or B?" the most frequent response given is "yes." The rabbis tend to want it both ways. Ask, "Is there freewill or predetermination?" The rabbis will answer, "All if foreseen but freewill is given." Ask, "Is God imminent (personal—in your heart) or transcended (universal—everywhere)?" The answer is again, "Yes, that's why God is God." And so it goes. In this section, we will understand how prayer is supposed to be both fixed and spontaneous.

In the Talmud, the rabbis talk about "stamping" or "minting" a *brakhah*. They were comparing the form of the *brakhah* to the size and pattern of coins that were stamped in metal. Even today, each coin has its own size and pattern. In rabbinic time, coins were one of the few manufactured items—things that were made exactly the same every time. Each stamped coin was identical. Most other items were handmade and each was unique. By labeling the pattern of a prayer the *matbeya tefillah* (the stamp of a prayer), the rabbis were showing us that Jewish prayer was designed to follow a very specific formula.

When the rabbis talked about prayer, they introduced two opposing notions: *keva* and *kavanah*.

*Keva* means fixed. It comes from a root that means "permanent." The idea of *keva* is that the words of the prayers are supposed to be the same; they are fixed permanent paths that guide our feelings. By "minting" *brakhot* and setting the pattern for worship, the rabbis were voting for *keva*.

*Kavanah* is the Hebrew word for "intention." It comes from a
root that means to "point" or "aim." The idea is that *kavanah* is
when you "aim your heart" and really mean something with all
your feelings. By accepting *brakhot* in other languages and in
other forms, the rabbis acknowledge that achieving the right
*kavanah* is indeed the essence of Jewish prayer.

What this talmudic debate really shows, however, is that the
rabbinic thought is different from ours. For them, *keva* was the
most predictable path to *kavanah*. While we live with a Western
bias toward the young and the new, they valued the rhythm
and pattern of a disciplined life-style. For them, the regimen-
tation of the word pattern gave freedom to those expressing
them—when you already know the path, you can pay attention
to the sights revealed along the way. That is why the rabbis
objected to "spiritual jay walking." Even if it is not dangerous
at 4:00 A.M., it doesn't create a path you can always follow.

# 3

# The Gift That Keeps
# On Giving

**The function of the *Barukh*—Part 1: From the Bible we learn that *brakhot* are "gifts" and "aspirations."**

Beginning with this chapter, we begin a word-for-word exploration of the *brakhah* formula, which will lead us through the next four chapters of this work. In this chapter, we will examine the biblical origins of the *brakhah*; in subsequent chapters we will follow these origins into their rabbinic adaption, followed by examinations of *Shem* and *Malkhut*.

## The Sneeze

Sneeze in Israel, and people will say *"la-bri'ut,"* "to your health." Do it in Germany, and the response is *"Gesundheit,"* also "Good health." In English we say, "God bless you." The truth is that all of these sneeze-response *brakhot* really are a shorthand for "You have just sneezed, you may be getting sick, may God bless you with good health."

The only blessing that is really part of our day-to-day life in

North America is the one that follows a sneeze. Go ahead, laugh, but after a sneeze is one of the few times that most modern North American people (especially Jews) will express positive feelings about God. In fact, it is one of the few times when we ever hear the word "bless" outside of a synagogue or church.

Interestingly, and I don't know how to fully explain it, "God bless you" is also the language of street people. Living in downtown Los Angeles, I spend a couple of dollars a day living up to Maimonides' dictum that a Jew (1) should never turn a beggar down and (2) should never give a beggar a significant amount of money. The usual response to receiving alms today is not "thank you," but "God bless you." And as I have learned from my friend and teacher, Trevor Farrel, the correct response is also, "God bless you, too." "You're welcome," is never part of the experience. It is not that kind of transaction. I have a hunch that this is what the *Gemara* is talking about in *Bava Batra* 10a:

> Rabbi Eliezer would give a coin to a beggar and then begin to pray. He would explain this practice by quoting Psalms 15:15:
>
> "Through *tzedakah* shall I see Your face (God)."

In other words, the "God bless you" of the street may be an intuitive response that this is a spiritual exchange, not a business transaction.

The interesting part of the "sneezing *brakhah*" is that it is really based on a core biblical concept: God is the source of blessings, so when people give blessings, they are really asking God to bless.

## Biblical *Brakhot*

Meet our guide to biblical *brakhot*: Abravanel. Sometimes it is helpful to have someone lead you through the biblical text and point out relevant points of interest. Abravanel will do that for us. Following his lead, we'll see that the Torah has three different meanings for the concept of *brakhot*. Each of them will influence our vision of prayer.

Abravanel was a Spanish biblical commentator who lived from 1437 to 1508, around the time of Columbus. He served as a finance minister to the kings of Portugal, Spain, and Naples. Exiled from Spain in 1492, he died in Venice.

When he looked at this problem (relative to the priestly benediction, Numbers 6:22–27), he explained biblical *brakhot* in this way:

*Brakhah* is a homonym (a word with three distinct meanings). It refers to:

a. the **good provided by God** to all God's creatures (as demonstrated by Genesis 24:1, "And *Adonai* blessed Abraham with all . . . "

b. the **praise directed to God** from people (as demonstrated by I Chronicles 29:10, "And David Blessed *Adonai* . . . "

c. *brakhot* **given by one person to another**—which should not be confused with the "gifts" provided by God, nor with statements of praise voiced by God's creatures, but rather as a request by the person speaking the blessing, that God provide for the person to be blessed.

Following Abravanel's lead, we'll examine these three types of biblical *brakhot*.

## Type 1 *Brakhot*: God to People

This is what happened right after God created people:

God blessed them—God said to them:

"Be Fruitful,
and become many,
and fill the earth,
and master it."

When God speaks, things happen. The first significant lesson in the Torah is that God creates through speaking. You know the pattern:

God said, "Let there be light."
And there was light.

What God says, comes to be. So, on the sixth day, when God immediately blesses people (just as soon as they are created), we learn that a blessing from God is a commitment, a promise that something will come to be. The extra phrase, "God said to them," proves it. If the text had just said, "God blessed them," it might just have been a wish. But once the Torah adds, "God said to them," there is no doubt—just like "Let there be light"—it must come to be.

Similarly, Jewish history begins in Chapter 12 of Genesis when God gives Abram this *brakhah*:

And I will make you a great nation
And I will bless you
And I will make your name great.
And you will be a blessing.
And I will bless those who bless you—
(And I will curse anyone who curses you)—
All the families of the earth will be blessed through you.

The rest of the Torah is the story of the fulfillment of this and later *brakhot*. Clearly, the things that Abram receives in this *brakhah* are gifts: family, fame, power, prosperity, etc. In subsequent blessings he is promised land. God, the Source of All *Brakhot*, is the Gift-Giver. And when the final *brakhah* is given, Abraham makes a response of thanksgiving. The Torah describes it in this way:

*Adonai* was seen by Abram.
*Adonai* Said:
"To your future-family I will give this land."

Abram built an altar
to *Adonai* Who is seen by him.

The lessons from this passage are twofold. First, when God gives a *brakhah*, God makes a **commitment**. A *brakhah* is an obligation to make something become true. Second, when Abram **receives** a *brakhah*, he says "**Thank you.**"[1]

From this first kind of *brakhah*, we learn two lessons:

a. "Saying" a *brakhah* is a **commitment** to make the wish it expresses come true.

b. **Receiving** a *brakhah* comes with the obligation to give **thanks**.

### Type 2 *Brakhot*: People to God

The first prayer in the Torah wasn't a *brakhah*; it was a straight request. When God confronts Cain after the murder of his brother, Cain cries out to God (Genesis 4:13):

My punishment is too great for me.
You have driven me out from the face of the land.
From Your face I shall be hidden.
I shall be a fugitive and a wanderer on the earth.
Whoever finds me may kill me . . .

When Abraham, Sarah, Isaac, Rebekah, Jacob, Rachel, Leah, and others wanted to express their gratitude to God, sacrifice was their medium. Most verbal exchanges between the patriarch/matriarchs and their God were petitions. One of the few specific biblical *brakhot* is found in 1 Chronicles 29:10. There, King David publicly blesses *Adonai*.

---

[1]From this passage, we also see a model that continues, until the time of the rabbis. People's gratitude to God was expressed through sacrifice—that is the reason for the absence of biblical texts that show us how to "bless" God. *Brakhot*, communal worship in particular, are part of the way the rabbis decentralized the role of the Temple and sacrifice in Jewish life.

> Blessed
> are You, *Adonai*,
> the God of Israel our father
> forever and ever.
> You, *Adonai*, are the greatness, and power, and the glory, and
>     victory, and the majesty
> for all that is in the heaven and the earth is Yours . . . .

The context here is that of a public assembly, a time when
David is handing his kingdom over to his son Solomon. This
public blessing is part of a group liturgy that culminates in
sacrifice. It is also, obviously, the sample that the rabbis used as
the model for the *brakhot* they authored.

We have already seen that the rabbinic *brakhah* formula
contains three elements: *Barukh*, *Shem*, and *Malkhut*. Those
same three "theme" elements can be found in David's prayer,
though with some variation (and a lot more words):

*Barukh*   = Praised

*Shem*      = are You, *Adonai*, the God of Israel our father
                    forever and ever.

*Malkhut* = You, *Adonai*, are the greatness, and power,
                    and the glory, and victory, and the majesty—
                    for all that is in the heaven and the earth is
                    Yours. . . .

This second category of biblical *brakhot* teaches us that:

a. *brakhot* are **responses to "gifts"** that God has given to us.
They are a liturgical way of saying "Thank You."

b. *brakhot* are both **private** and **public expressions** of gratitude.
Both the private "pleasure-*brakhah*" response and the public
"worship-*brakhah*" pattern have roots in biblical practice.

c. when the rabbis came to create the *brakhah* system, they
pattern the *brakhah* formula and a biblical pattern, retaining
the *Barukh* and shortening the *Shem* section, while reworking the *Malkhut*.

## Type 3 *Brakhot*: People to People.

The last kind of *brakhah* pattern comes when people bless others, especially their children. One of the prime examples happens when Isaac blesses Jacob with a *brakhah* overtly intended for Esau (Genesis 27:27 ff):

> See, the smell of my son is like the smell of a field
> that *Adonai* has blessed.
> May God give you from the dew of the sky
> and the richness of the earth
> and much grain and new wine.
> May nations serve you and may peoples bow to you.
> Be master over your brother
> and may the sons of your mother bow to you.
> Let those who curse you be cursed.
> Let those who bless you be blessed.

This blessing doesn't remind us of *ha-Motzi* (over bread) or *Kiddush* (over wine). It doesn't resemble our usual human *brakhot*. When God blesses a person, God is making promises about that person's future. When God gives a *brakhah*, God changes a person's life. When people bless each other, they wish for God's *brakhah*. Isaac, here, uses the "sneeze-*brakhah*" concept and asks God to bless his son.

Perhaps this is most clearly tested in the famous "priestly *brakhot*" taught in Numbers 6:22–27.

> *Adonai* spoke to Moses saying:
> Speak to Aaron and to his sons, saying:
> This is how you will bless the Families of Israel, saying:
>
> "May *Adonai* bless you and keep you.
> May *Adonai* make God's face shine upon you
> and be kind to you.
> May *Adonai* let God's face turn to you
> and give you peace."
>
> And they shall put My name on the Families of Israel,
> and I will bless them.

The last sentence, "And they shall put My name on the Families of Israel, and I will bless them," confused those who tried to explain this passage. The standard question was, "If God is doing the blessing, why does God have the priests put the Name on the people?" God shouldn't need a "homing device" to know who to bless (God's *brakhot* should be "smart *brakhot*"—laser targeted). The problem gets solved in a number of different ways. Each solution suggests something else about the process of blessing.

## Solution 1

In the Talmud, *Hullin* 48a, we find this solution.

> "And I will bless them" refers to the sons of Aaron; the *kohanim* (priests) bless Israel and The Holy-One-Who-Is-to-Be-Blessed blesses them.

Grammatically, the solution is elegant—however, theologically it creates problems. It gives people the power to bless other people, rather than just invoking God's blessing.

The rabbis, however, offered other solutions.

## Solution 2

In *Midrash Tanhuma*, an early collection of *midrashim*, we find this passage:

> The Families of Israel said to The Holy-One-Who-is-to-Be-Blessed, "The Ruler-of-the-Cosmos, why did you order the *kohanim* to bless us? We need only Your *brakhah*. Please look down from Your Holy habitation and bless Your people.

> The Holy-One-Who-is-to-be-Blessed answered Israel. Even though I ordered the *kohanim* to bless you, I stand with them and together We bless you.

This solution offers a wonderful understanding. People can offer blessings, and God can assure them. While a human *brakhah* cannot be a guarantee, a perfect promise, it is still a wonderful gift. God wants us to have the opportunity to offer such gifts and to strive to enact their truthfulness.

## Solution 3

Abravanel, the Spanish commentator whose explanation of this verse we have used to organize this passage, takes the hardest line:

> There are also *brakhot* **given by one person to another**—which should not be confused with the "gifts" provided by God, nor with statements of praise voiced by God's creatures, but rather as a request by the person speaking the blessing that God provide for the person to be blessed. The priestly *brakhot* fall into this last category.

For Abravanel, humans have no role in the granting of *brakhot*—they can only request them.[2]

## Review:

**The problem:** What is the meaning of the verse, "And they (the *kohanim*) shall put My name on the Families of Israel, and I

---

[2]A process note: This short analysis of the priestly *brakhot* and the meanings they have had in the rabbinic tradition models something important for us. It shows, first, that Jewish text study is rooted in finding the questions inherent in the texts themselves—in this case, the contradiction between "And they shall put My name on the Families of Israel," which suggests that the *kohanim* are the ones doing the blessing, and "And I will bless them," which suggests that God is the one doing the blessing. What follows are, of course, three distinct solutions to the question found in the text: the first, which grants the *kohanim* the power to bless; the second, which suggests that God can co-officiate and empower their *brakhot*; and the third, which suggests that people can only request *brakhot* from God. The "process" lesson is that Jewish study centers around significant questions around which we can collect and evolve a number valid answers.

(God) will bless them"? Who is the "them"? Is God blessing the *kohanim* or the people? And, if God is blessing the people, what is the *kohanim's* role and function? In other words, "Can a person *give* a *brakhah*, or only *ask* for a *brakhah*?"

**Solution 1—The Talmud,** *Hullin* **48a**: The *kohanim* have the power to bless the people (and God in turn blesses the *kohanim*). Because Israel is "a kingdom of *kohanim*," Jews have the power to grant *brakhot*.

**Solution 2—***Midrash Tanhuma*: Jews have the power to grant blessings with God's help. God is disposed to help *brakhot* offered by Jews to come true.

**Solution 3—Abravanel**: *Brakhot* are only requests. It is up to God to see that they come true.

## Conclusions

Some of you, dear readers, may wonder why there is this long diversion through biblical exegesis. There are really two reasons. First, the more you enter the world of the rabbis, the clearer the *siddur's* pattern of ideas will become. Second, and more importantly, we have actually built a solid foundation for our understanding of the spiritual process of saying a *brakhah*.

1. For God, *brakhot* are a **commitment**. When God gives a *brakhah*, God insures that this *brakhah* will come true. Because we are created in God's image, striving to live up to that image, our *brakhot* should also be **commitments**.

2. When people say a *brakhah*, it can and should be a **statement of radical appreciation**, an expression of gratitude and praise.

3. When people give a *brakhah*, it can also be a **wish**, a hope that something will become true.

4. If we read the Torah through the eyes of *Midrash Tanhuma*, this very act of "wishing" a *brakhah* may well be **the first step in its actualization**.

These ideas teach us something about our saying *brakhot*. *Brakhot* for us are clearly **statements of radical appreciation**. We acknowledge what God has done for us. But, they are also **wishes** and **commitments**. As we read the rabbinic material in the following chapter, we will see that, using the biblical idea that people were created in God's image, the rabbis had us understand that when we said a *brakhah* and thanked God for giving us a **gift**, we had a **wish** to be like God and a wish to give similar gifts to others. Our saying the *brakhah* is a **commitment** to do everything we can to make that **wish** come true.

## P.S.

We have also learned that giving *tzedakah* may teach us something about how to pray.

# 4

# Imitation Is the Sincerest Form of Blessing

**The function of the *Barukh*—Part 2: From the rabbis we learn that saying *brakhot* is like: jumping in a pool, bowing, and saying "thank you."**

## Metaphor 1: The Pool

What is it like to jump into a pool?

*It starts with a shock—everywhere. There is cold. All nerves tingle and shout: Yes, you are awake. Even if you were awake, now you are really awake. The shock of cold and wet brings radical awareness. Parts of your body that you haven't thought about in days (or at least hours) are suddenly calling for attention. They are having an "experience" and they now want to be noticed.*

*Also, you are completely immersed. In a sense you are now floating, not standing. Your body is being carried and is somewhat off center. You kick and stroke, moving to find the surface.*

*Next, you get an urgent message. Your lungs remind you that your* body is no longer running on auto-breath; the system is now on manual and it is awaiting instructions. Soon, you will need to take another breath.

Within seconds, the internal gyroscope kicks in. Up is just above the quivering boundary between water and air. Head pointed, feet kicking, you shoot toward the light. Your face breaks the surface, water streams down, you throw your head back, you toss the hair out of your eyes, and you scream, just to express the sense of being envigorated and of feeling fully alive.

Jumping into a pool is being startled into radical awareness, being immersed, directing yourself, breaking the surface, and feeling fully alive.

## What is it like to draw water out of a well?

The bucket drops into the deep dark shaft. The bottom is somewhere beyond your vision, but you sense that it is dropping toward the source. Down, far below the surface, the water runs dark and cold. The well shaft lets you tap into this buried life-source.

The bucket hits the water and you sense the connection—the rope stops unwinding. Then, in a series of turns and pulls, this life fluid is brought back. Slowly, what had been hidden down deep emerges into view.

You drink the cool water. You feel it enter your body and flow inside you. The refreshment spreads. You feel the renewal. There is a sense of "ahhhh!"

Drinking water from a well is reaching down to the source, sensing the connection, taking the water inside, and feeling it renew you.

### Rabbinic Synectics

בְּרֵכָה *breikhah* = **a pool or well**
בְּרָכָה *brakhah* = **a blessing**

The Hebrew word for a pool or a well is a בְּרֵכָה *breikhah*. It shares the same three letter root [ברך] as *brakhah*. In a piece of *midrash*, the rabbis expressed a connection.

Synectics[1] is a problem-solving system that uses metaphors. It asks how one thing is like another. In this case, the question would be, "How is a *brakhah* (blessing) like a *breikhah* (pool/well)?" When I am teaching, I ask it as, "How is saying a *brakhah* like jumping into a pool? How is saying a *brakhah* like drinking from a well?" The rabbis of the *midrash* used the conjunction of the form of *breikhah* and *brakhah* for their own synectics exercise. We'll get to their understanding later in this chapter.

## A Tangent: What is *Midrash*?

The *midrash* is a literature of biblical explanations that grew from an oral process into a precise written form. When Jews first returned to the Land of Israel from the Babylonian Exile (ca. 500 B.C.E.), Ezra, the religious leader of the community, instituted a number of reforms. Two, among them, were (1) reading the Torah publicly on Mondays and Thursdays, and (2) providing an Aramaic translation (the daily language) to accompany the Hebrew reading. Soon, the translators (as all translators do) began adding interpretations alongside the translations. Eventually, they changed their job description. The *meturgaman* (translator) became the *darshan* (explainer/sermon giver). And in the long run, these explanations evolved into an art form we now call *midrash*. By and large, as we have already seen, when the rabbis come to explain a Jewish concept, they prefer to build it from biblical roots. The process they usually use is *midrash*.

## The Biblical Source

One of the prime explanations of what happens when a person says a *brakhah* (of how a *brakhah* is like a *breikhah*) is built

---

[1]My friend and teacher, Gail Dorph, got interested a few years ago in a brainstorm process called "synectics." Ultimately, she shared the technique with many of us, and we in turn use it as a teaching strategy.

on the story of God's first covenant with Abram in chapter 12
of Genesis. There God makes the first promises to the first Jew.
God gives this *brakhah*:

> And I will make you a great nation.
> And I will **bless** you.
> And I will make your name great.
> And you will be a **blessing**.
> And I will **bless** those who **bless** you.
> (And I will curse anyone who curses you)—
> All the families of the earth will be **blessed** through you.

Read this biblical passage and the word *blessing* stands out.
So do some questions. "I will bless you" is somewhat obvious.
We already have studied the notion that blessings are gifts
given by God. Therefore, the following two blessing promises,
which make Abraham a source of blessings, seem confusing.
"You will be a blessing" is hard to conceptualize as something
concrete. So is "All the families of the earth will be blessed
through you." The passage stands in need of explanation. How
can a person "be" a blessing (especially if God is the source of
*brakhah*)? How can all families be blessed through one person?
One of the places the rabbis take up this challenge is in *Genesis
Rabbah* 39:11 (the eleventh *midrash* in the the thirty-ninth
chapter of the collection of Genesis *midrashim* known as "the
great collection").

## The Midrashic Analysis

### a.

Rabbi Levi said, "No person ever priced a cow belonging to
Abraham [in order to buy it] without becoming blessed. No one
ever priced a cow [in order to sell it] to Abraham without
becoming blessed.

Abraham used to pray for barren women and they were
remembered [by God and became pregnant], on behalf of the
sick, and they were healed.

Rabbi Levi's solution here is actually quite subtle. Much of its artistry hides beneath its surface. In the biblical text there are two promises that stand in need of explanation: "You will be a blessing" and "All the families of the earth will be blessed through you." Rabbi Levi's *midrash* explains not only what they each mean, but also what the difference is between them. By doing the latter, he shows why God gave both promises.[2] "You will be a blessing" means (according to Rabbi Levi) that interacting with Abraham was good for business. If you did business with him, both you and he prospered. At the same time, Rabbi Levi gives an almost literal explanation of "All the families of the earth will be blessed through you." For him, Abraham's concern could help women conceive and bear the greatest *brakhah*, a child. Likewise, his attention could induce God to heal the sick. In this *midrash*, he literally becomes the catalyst for family blessings, bringing them children (and making them families) and sustaining them as families by healing their members. Therefore, each promise in the *brakhah* has a clear and distinct purpose.

### b.

Following Rabbi Levi's explanation, the *midrash* continues with two other versions of the miraculous nature of Abraham's blessing. Often, *midrash*-making seems like a game of "topper," the kind of storytelling session where each participant tries to

---

[2]For the rabbis, God was the sole author of the Torah. Because the Torah was Divine, it had to represent perfect communication. That meant (among other things) no superfluous or extraneous material, nothing extra. In this case, if two of the promises given by God to Abram were the same, one of them would be redundant (and therefore un-Godlike). Therefore, we can assume (because God did write the Torah) that each promise in this blessing represents something different, and our task in understanding this passage is to establish the unique message of each part. If you've followed this footnote, you are now well on your way to mastering midrashic thinking.

"outdo" the person who had "gone" previously. In a game of topper, each contestant starts with the ritual formula: "That's nothing. . . ." As this sequence in the *midrash* continues, the miraculous nature of Abraham's *brakhah*-giving skill expands.

> Rav Huna said, "[That's nothing . . . ] Abraham didn't need to go and actually visit the sick person, [because] once the sick person saw him, he or she was cured."

> Rav Hanina said, "[That's nothing . . . ] even ships traveling the sea were saved [through his existence].

### c.

Then, continuing in a new direction with this same process, the next section of this passage compares Abraham and Job. Another rabbinic tendency, trained by years of listening to the style of biblical narrative, is the cross-referencing of passages. When the rabbis read one verse, they automatically begin to think of other verses in the Bible that use similar words and phrases. Often, by comparing the two, the rabbis unlock more of the meaning of word-concept that connects them. That is what is happening in this next piece of *midrash*.

> Rav Yitzhak said, "God gave the same kind of *brakhah* to Job. There, [in Chapter 1, verse 10,] it says: 'You [God] have blessed the work of his [Job's] hands.' No one who accepted a penny from Job [in *tzedakah* or in business] ever had to take a second one from him."

This comparison with Job is important. Only three people in the Bible are described as being righteous: Noah, Abraham, and Job. Only Abraham and Job were considered "totally righteous" (or close to totally righteous). Therefore, if the *brakhah* formula can be connected to both of them, we have learned an important lesson. What Rav Yitzhak is teaching, but not overtly saying, in his comment is that God gives *brakhot* to people who act righteously, and their life, in turn, benefits those with whom they interact. In other words, righteous people really do make a difference. By making the comparison with Job, Rav Yitzhak is showing that it is Abraham's righteous actions that are at the heart of this blessing.

d.

Finally, after this series of explorations, the *midrash* comes to the piece that originally attracted our attention:

And You Shall Be a Blessing [*Brakhah*]: this means you will be like a *breikhah* [pool]. In the same way that a pool purifies the unclean, so you bring near [to Me] people who are far away.

This anonymous bit of *midrash* brings us closer to the essence we seek. It shifts us from *brakhot* being gifts to *brakhot* being a spiritual process. Here, Abraham, who is a living *brakhah*, brings a *brakhah* to those with whom he interacts—but this time the nature of the *brakhah* has changed: (1) For Rabbi Levi, a *brakhah* was prosperity, progeny, and health (a fairly literal biblical definition, based on what we learned in the previous section). (2) For Rav Huna and Rav Hanina, the *brakhah* was beyond the normal ability to gain these things; it was a miraculous propensity toward them. (3) For Rav Yitzhak, the *brakhah* was a payment (of the Rabbi Levi magnitude) as a reward for righteous action. (4) But, for this last anonymous position, a *brakhah* was the ability to get close to God, to experience the Divine.[3]

---

[3]Behind this last midrashic comment is the idea of *teshuvah*, repentance. It is not so hidden in the phrase "pool that purifies the unclean." *Teshuvah* means "return," and it symbolizes the return from doing wrong and the reestablishment of the original relationship between God and a person, a rapprochement. So what is being said in this piece of *midrash* is that being (or saying) a *brakhah* has the potential to achieve *teshuvah* and to reconnect people to God.

That idea is not only found here. Samson Raphael Hirsch, the great nineteenth-century Orthodox thinker, basing himself (in a midrashic way) on I Samuel 2:23 matched against Exodus 22:8, defines prayer as

The initial implication of the *midrashic* approach to *brakhot* is twofold:

1. We are directed to find a connection between saying/being *brakhot* and ethical action.

2. The being/saying of *brakhot* is in some way designed to bring us (and others) close to God (again).[4]

## From All My Students I Have Gained Wisdom

For several years now, I have made my students into "instant" rabbis and left them the task of making synectic *midrashim* connecting blessings, pools, and wells. Sages ranging from age nine to age sixty-three (or so) have taught me the following:

> Like jumping into a pool, saying a *brakhah* shocks you into paying attention.
> Like jumping into a pool, saying a *brakhah* immerses you totally.
> Like jumping into a pool, saying a *brakhah* forces you to find a way (back) up.
> Like jumping into a pool, saying a *brakhah* can really wake you up.
> Like drinking from a well, saying a *brakhah* brings you something from The Source.

---

self-judgment. He says, "Certainly, there is sufficient, reasonable cause for a person to take stock of herself several times a day, or to bring himself to trial, to examine her actions, to determine whether he conforms to the ideal. . . ."

[4]Before we leave this flow of *midrashim*, there are two other small fragments that are interesting to mention. Sometimes, the *Midrash* is wonderfully literal. In this same section, *Genesis Rabbah* 39:11, the rabbis explain "I will make your name great" as being fulfilled in the transformation of "Abram" into "Abraham" (a bigger name). And they explain that "You will be a blessing" is fulfilled by the *Avot* prayer, the *brakhah* that begins the *Amidah*. Abraham is mentioned in the first and last line of that *brakhah*.

Like drinking from a well, saying a *brakhah* refreshes and renews
   you.
Like drinking from a well, saying a *brakhah* is something you
   need.
Like drinking from a well, saying a *brakhah* is a reward.

The lesson here is that making of *midrash* (yes, the method of
metaphor) is sometimes a valuable way of coming to describe
an abstract process.[5]

## Metaphor 2: The Knees

**When do we bend our knees? What does it feel like? What
does it teach us?**

*Think about bending your knees. Where are you? The gym?
Changing a tire? Holding up Ginger Rogers? Meeting Queen Latisha?
(No, I don't know who Queen Latisha is either—but this is your
fantasy!) From all your experience of knee bending, what does it mean?*

בֶּרֶךְ *berekh* = knee
בְּרָכָה *brakhah* = a blessing

The Hebrew word for knee is *berekh*. It, too, like *brakhah*, is
built around the three letter root [ברך]. Obviously, there is a
connection. In the next section of *Genesis Rabbah*, 39:12, the
rabbis explore this metaphor. There, paralleling a talmudic
discussion found in *Brakhot* 34a, the rabbis establish the connection, though they do not make it explicit.

Basically, it comes down to a simple idea. A person bends a

---

[5]It also shows, I think, something that I have long believed to be
true. Rabbinic Judaism, particularly *midrash*, is something that every
generation can, to a large degree, re-create. Like DNA chains, the
string of potential interpretations seems imbedded in the biblical text,
ready to reproduce themselves whenever the critical questions are
asked.

knee (bows) before seeing royalty. God, who is the Ruler-of-Rulers, is the ultimate royalty. Saying a *brakhah* to God is like bending a knee before a queen or king, an acknowledgment of authority and position. In fact, some *brakhot* are said with knee bends being part of the choreography.

Ironically, my students (especially my adult students) see this completely differently, and in their own way echoed a teaching of Philo, a famous Jewish philosopher who lived in Alexandria, Egypt, sometime around the year 40 C.E. He taught that Jews were ethical athletes (he was really into the Greco-Roman thing) and that prayer was their daily training regimen. My students, being Americans, never bowed to royalty. For them, bending the knee was a gym activity done after jumping jacks and before squat thrusts. When asked to explain its connection to *brakhot*, blessings became spiritual exercises. Not bad!

## Conclusions

The word *barukh*, which begins each *brakhah*, is actually an adjective. It defines God as "*Barukh*," e.g., The Source-of-all-*Brakhot*.

Yet, in a formative, nongrammatical way, the word *barukh* triggers an action, a process of "*barukh*-ing." It is this quest for "what the *brakhah* does" for the person saying it that is behind our search through this rabbinic material.

In the section on biblical *brakhot* we learned that:

a. The foundational understanding of *brakhot* is that they are **gifts** given to people by God. They are promises, about their future, which just by speaking, God makes come true.

b. Likewise, *brakhot* offered by one person to another are essentially **wishes** that God will provide them with *brakhah*.

c. Finally, *brakhot* said by people to God are **acknowledgments** of the gifts that they had received—a liturgical thank you.

However, starting with the rabbinic analysis of the priestly *brakhot*, we begin to see some other meanings of *brakhah*. By working through the clues found in rabbinic discussions of biblical *brakhot*, we begin to learn some other things.

d. By making a *brakhah*, it is possible for a person to stand in **partnership** with God, helping to insure the **actualization** of the wish. (This is the explanation given by *Midrash Tanhuma* to the priests' involvement in blessing the people.)

e. The process of living a *brakhah* (making its meaning true), which is, indeed, truly saying it, is a process of **ethical living**—righteousness. (This is the insight found in Rabbi Yitzhak's comparison of Job and Abraham.)

f. Being a *brakhah* (living out the said words) is a process of finding that part **inside yourself** that connects you to and lets you feel close to God (the teaching of the anonymous *midrash* about the pool).

In these three rabbinic insights, we begin to see a sense of what it means to "do" *brakhah* rather than just "receive" or "acknowledge" *brakhah*. *Brakhah*, in this sense, has a potential to serve as an agent of change, rather than as a verbal transaction. One additional biblical idea helps to focus all of these elements and provides us with a simple, and highly teachable model.

## *Brakhot* and God's Image

In the first chapter of Genesis, we learn of the creation of people. There we learn this lesson:

God said: "Let Us make people in **Our image**.
Let them rule over the fish and the birds,
over the beasts and the creeping things."
God made people in **God's image**.
God created people—both man and woman.

For the Jewish tradition, the notion of being created in God's image is an ethical lesson, not a physiological one. God's image means "we can act in Godlike ways," not "we look like God." I find it explained best in the real-life "hasidic" story of my friend Levi Kelman, who was raised as the son of a significant Conservative teacher within the community of the Jewish Theological Seminary.

> A boy named Levi was talking with his father. The father told Levi that God was invisible.
> Levi asked his father, "If God is invisible, can God see God?"
> His father thought a long while. He then asked Levi, "When you want to see yourself, where do you look?"
> Levi answered his father, "In the mirror."
> Then Levi's father said, "When God wants to see God's image, God looks at you, to see it in the best of what you do."[6]

### Imitation is the Sincerest Form of *Brakhah*

From the Bible we know that *brakhot* are really **gifts** from God and that human *brakhot* are either (or both) **wishes** for more blessings or **acknowledgment** of existing blessings. However, at the heart of the rabbinic transformation of this idea of *brakhot* is the notion of "God's image." If I am truly grateful for something done for me, and I truly respect The Giver, the best way of showing my gratitude (of living out my thanks) is to emulate The Giver. I return the kindness done my parents by passing on the love to my own children, and so on. Striving to imitate God and to live up to God's image is the essence of becoming a *brakhah*. Clearly, the goal of saying *brakhot* (according to the authors of these *brakhot*) is to internalize them and become them. Jews are ultimately interested in being *brakhot*; saying them is a developmental step.

Therefore "*barukh*-ing," the act of saying *brakhot* in order to become *brakhot*, is:

----

[6]This version of the Levi Kelman story is found in my book *Being Torah* (Los Angeles: Torah Aura Productions, 1985).

1. Focusing my attention and noticing the **gifts** that I received from God.

2. Being grateful and **acknowledging** them, thanking God for those gifts.

3. **Wishing** that I can become more like God, and **helping** to actualize these same gifts for other people.

4. **Committing** myself to do everything in my power to make this wish come true, the same way God makes God's *brakhot* come true.

5. **Connecting** to those places inside of me that bring me close to God, inspiring and empowering my actions.

This description of *"barukh-ing"* is a functional description of the process of Jewish prayer. All this is embedded in one word: *Barukh*.

# 5

# *Adonai* Is a Name, Like "Fred"—God Is a Job Description, Like "A Lawyer"

**The function of the *Shem*—Part 1: The use of God's Name— *Adonai*—is like dialing the family God.**

## A Prologue: A Postmodern *Midrash*

I am יהוה *Adonai*.
I appeared to Abraham, Isaac, and Jacob as אֵל שַׁדַּי *El Shaddai* (God from On High),
But I did not make Myself known by My Name יהוה *Adonai*
                                        Exodus 6:2

Mar Joel, son of Isaac, taught, "To what can this be compared?"

"To a corporate executive who said to her children, 'This is my private phone number, one that not even your father knows. If you are in trouble, use it to reach me—it doesn't go through any switch board—it is a direct line.'

"'And, by the way,' she also said, 'use it to call me every day, just so I know how you are doing.'"

51

## The Conclusion

In this section we are going to look at the unique connotations of the God name *Adonai*. Because I have already hinted at much of what we will learn, we are going to begin this section with our conclusions—using the rest of these pages to fully establish and deepen these ideas.

1. Jews believe that there are two different categories of religious experiences.

   That is another way of saying that there are two distinct paths by which a person can connect with the Divine. One of these is intimate, particularly Jewish, and personal. The other is transcended, universal, and in a real sense cosmic.

2. *Adonai* is God's name. (Actually, *Adonai* is God's nickname, a place holder for יהוה).

   It expresses one of these two spiritual possibilities, that is, the intimate, particularly Jewish, personal religious experience available to Jews via their covenant with the God of Jewish history.

3. The *Shem* part of the *brakhah* formula not only includes God's name but also the word "You."

   It is in the second person and suggests that our relationship with God as *Adonai* is a kind of "face-to-face" encounter.

## A Review: *Adonai* Is God's Name

We have already looked at this text, but we must return to it, because it is our starting point. It is the monologue God speaks to Moses shortly after the burning bush incident:

I am יהוה *Adonai*.
I appeared to Abraham, Isaac, and Jacob as אֵל שַׁדָּי *El Shaddai* (God from On High),
But I did not make Myself known by My Name יהוה *Adonai*

I also established My covenant with them
to give them the land of Canaan . . . .

יהוה (as we have said before) is God's actual name, not a title,
not a description. The rabbis tried not to use God's name and
therefore chose to call God by such attributes as: The Holy-
One-Who-Is-to-Be-Blessed, The One-Who-Spoke-and-the- Cos-
mos-Came-to-Be, The-Merciful-One. It is therefore noteworthy
that they chose not only to include but to demand the use of
God's name in every *brakhah*.[1]

The name, represented by these four letters (and for that
reason also called the Tetragrammaton, the "four lettered
name"), was treated completely differently and was avoided in
most contexts. It is that very avoidance that gives us such place
holders as Lord[2] and *Adonai*, which in turn have their own
place holders: *ha-Shem*, G-d, and even in some cases, L-rd. It is
that very tendency toward avoidance that makes its mandatory
presence in the *brakhah* formula so important.

This unique importance is what we will explore in both this
and the next part of this chapter. The significance of *Adonai*, the
Name, is something that can only be clarified through con-
trasting it with *Elohim*, another God name.

## The Difference between "Lord" and "God"

### The Biblical Beginning

The Torah begins this way:

Beginnings:
**God** created the heavens and the earth.
The earth was unformed and chaotic.

---

[1]That is the final conclusion reached as consensus in *Brakhot* 40b.

[2]The word *Lord* is another one of the place-holding substitutes for
the four-lettered name of God. It has commonly been used as the
English translation of this God name, while not at all reflecting its
actual meaning. Ironically, it emphasizes (using sexist terminology)
God's regal aspects, rather than God's paternal aspects—*Adonai*'s
actual connotation.

> Darkness was over the deep.
> The breath of **God** was over the waters.
> **God** said, "Let there be light."
> And there was light.
> And **God** saw that the light was good.

The initial deity of creation is *Elohim*, a Hebrew word for God. *Elohim* is not really a name (though in practice it has become one); it is really a job description. Both the one Jewish God (*Adonai*) and all of the pagan gods are labeled as *Elohim*. Sometimes, as we will learn later, even human judges are called *Elohim*.

Starting in the second half of verse four of the second chapter of Genesis, the Torah again begins to tell the story of the creation of the universe. It is as if we have shifted camera angles. This time the story is told from a different focus. Whereas the first account of creation (the "Let there be light" version) is concerned with the cosmic order of creation, the second story (The "Garden of Eden" version) is concerned with the relationship between God and people. It begins this way:

> This is the family history of the heavens and the earth from their
>     creation.
> On the day when the **God**, *Adonai*, made earth and heaven,
> there were no bushes and there were no plants growing,
> because the **God**, *Adonai*, had not yet made rain.
> There was no human to till the soil.
> The **God**, *Adonai*, formed Adam from the dust of the soil
> and breathed into his nose the breath of life.
> Adam came Alive.

If you've begun to read with rabbinic eyes (or if you've picked up my not-so-subtle use of text prompting), the following question should have made itself manifest:

> Why do the two stories use two different references to God? In
>     other words, why did *Adonai* get added to *Elohim* in the
>     second story?

## Reading with Rashi

Our guide to unraveling this particular biblical enigma is Rabbi Shlomo ben Yitzhak, also known as Rashi:

When Jews struggle with the meaning of a given biblical problem, there are many places to look for solutions, but their first stop is usually Rashi. Rashi is the acronym for **R**abbi **Sh**lomo **Y**itzhaki (Yitzhaki = Ben Yitzhak), a famous eleventh-century French scholar, whose commentaries on both the Bible and the Talmud are considered to be the "traditional" first guide for any Jewish exploration. What Rashi often does, especially when he comments on the Bible, is summarize the essence of the rabbinic opinions found in the Talmud and the *Midrash*. In that way he provides easy access to the long-term Jewish view of a passage.

When the Torah says, "On the day when the **God,** *Adonai,* made earth and heaven," Rashi adds this brief note:

> יהוה (*Adonai*) is God's [actual] name. אֱלֹהִים (*Elohim*) means that God is Ruler and Judge[3] over all. Therefore, whenever the two [God names] appear together, the plain meaning is: "*Adonai,* Who is God (Ruler and Judge)."

Here, Rashi is drawing on a long-standing rabbinic assumption, the belief that *Adonai* and *Elohim* (God) represent different, distinct attributes of God.

The contrast between *Adonai* and *Elohim* (God) in Rashi reveals more than a simple distinction. Remember, we began our exploration with the question, "Why does the Torah introduce the second creation story (the "Garden of Eden"

---

[3]In the following part we will establish that the Hebrew *Elohim* stands for God's aspect of judgment. It must be understood that this is not a rabbinic whim, but an actual extension of biblical language. At several points in the biblical text, the word *Elohim* is clearly used as the words *human judges*—a power source, if you will. The reapplication of this idea of judging back to God is a logical extension of their close reading.

version) with two God names? So far, we can easily explain that *Elohim*, the Judgment God, who represents God The Creator, is the right choice for the formalized day-by-day, well-ordered creation story. And it is equally easy to suggest that *Adonai*, the personal Friendly God with a first name, is the right choice for the Divinity in the story where God talks frequently and personally with Adam and Eve. However, one key question that remains unresolved is, "Why does the second story use *both* names?" At first glance, Rashi has ignored the issue. However, when we look into the *midrash* (*Genesis Rabbah* 12:15), the probable source Rashi was summarizing (and in a sense, cluing us to examine), the resolution becomes clear.

## Rashi's Roots: Justice and Mercy

**"*Adonai*, the God, made earth and heaven."**

This can be compared to a king who had some empty glasses. Said the king, "If I pour hot water into them, they will burst; if I pour cold water into them, they will contract and snap." So, what did the king do? He mixed hot and cold water and poured it into them, so they remained unbroken.

This is just what The Holy-One-Who-Is-to-Be-Blessed said. "If I create the world on the basis of *mercy* alone, its sins will be great. If I create it on the basis of *justice* alone, the world cannot exist. Hence I will create it on both the basis of judgment and the basis of mercy, and then it may stand!" Therefore, the Torah teaches *Adonai*, the God (*Elohim*).

It is from here we learn that *Adonai* represents God's approachable aspect, *midat ha-rahamin*—**the attribute of mercy**; and *Elohim* (the Judge) represents God's absolute aspect *midat ha-din*—**the attribute of justice**. Classically, rabbinic literature speaks of "aspects of God"; in modern parlance, "experiences of God" probably has more meaning.

In a real sense, the rabbis are extrapolating the well-known

story of the three blind men who encounter an elephant. Each
has a different experience of the elephant and each describes it
differently. The first says, "An elephant is like a tree." The
second says, "An elephant is like a rope." The third says, "An
elephant is like a roof." Just as the each blindman's experience
of the elephant is limited by the aspect that is closest to him, so
our experience of God is limited by the nature of the actual
encounter. No one has the vision to see God as a whole—
certainly not at once.[4] Therefore, while rabbinic categories
center on the nature of God, in our time it is equally logical to
describe such diversity in terms of the feelings and experiences
of God.

The "secret message" at the center of this *midrash* is one that
we will find important later on. People (including Jews) need to
relate to both *Adonai* and *Elohim*. It takes both aspects to
complete our relationship with God, and both aspects are
important parts of the image of God we are seeking to
incorporate into our actions. Therefore, the inclusion of both
*Shem* (the mention of *Adonai*) and *Malkhut* (our relationship
with the cosmic *Elohim*) are necessary parts of our prayer
process.

In *Exodus Rabbah* 3:6 (the "Big Collection of *Midrashim* on
Exodus") commenting on God's explanation of the the name
יהוה, "I am that I am!" we find this *midrash*, which further
clarifies the name distinctions:

Rabbi Abba ben Memel said:

"God said to Moses, 'So you want to know My Name. Use the
name that fits My actions. When I judge my creatures, I am

---

[4]In the Talmud, *Ta'anit* 15b, it says, "One who repeats something
in the name of the person who said it hastens the redemption. It is a
wonderful rabbinic notion that footnoting the "Chain of the Tradition" is a messianic process. It is why the Talmud is filled with "Rabbi
So-and-So said in the name of Rabbi So-and-So . . . . " In this case, I
have no idea of the origins of the this particular folk story (which is
probably Indian in origin), but I do remember first learning it as a
creative writing exercise given by my seventh grade English teacher,
Mrs. Lape.

called *Elohim*. When I wage war against the wicked, I am called
*Tzevaot*, when I suspend judgment for a person's sins, I am
called *El Shaddai*, but when I have compassion on the world, I
am called *Adonai*. *Adonai* is the attribute of mercy, as it is taught
in Exodus 34:6, "*Adonai, Adonai* is merciful and gracious." "I am
that I am" means I am named by My actions.'"

## Creator and Revealer

The split between The God-of-Mercy and The God-of-Justice
is only one of the contrasts the rabbis found. Another was
revealed in Psalm 19.

The heavens number the honor of *Elohim*
The sky tells of the work of *His* hands
Every day speaks praise
Every night reveals knowledge . . . .

Psalm 19:2–3

*Adonai*'s Torah is perfect—renewing the soul.
*Adonai*'s testimony is true—making wise the simple
*Adonai*'s laws are right—making the heart happy
*Adonai*'s *mitzvot* are pure—enlightening the eyes . . . .

Psalm 19:8–9

Here, a different contrast becomes obvious, one we fore-
shadowed earlier.

*Elohim* is God, The Creator, The One-Who-Fixed-the-Universe-
in-Its-Precise-Order, The God-Who-Makes-Things-Exact (and
Who therefore is God, The Precise-and-Exacting-Uncompro-
mising-Judge).

Adonai is God, the Revealer, The One-Who-Gave-Torah-to-
God's-People, the God-Who-Teaches-and-Patiently-Reteaches-
Israel, the God-Who-Slowly-and-with-Much-Forgiveness-Gives-
Us-Many-Second-Chances-to-Try-to-Live-by-the-Torah.

For a long time, I found the connection between *Adonai* and Torah a hard connection to make. I always associated Torah with law and law with judgment. That is a Western set of associations. For the rabbis, Torah is an act of love. It is important to think of the Torah, not just as a book of rules, but also as the story of all of our second chances. For example:

> Adam and Eve eat from the tree, but God gives them a way to start over.
> Cain kills Abel, but God allows him to go on living.
> People are evil, but after the Flood, God helps humanity to rebuild.
> People build the Tower of Babel, and while babbling their languages, God sends them off to start again.
> When humanity as a group clearly will fail to live ethically, God chooses Abraham's family to be a "prototype people"[5] (classically, a light to the nations).
> When Israel rejects the Torah and accepts the golden calf, God adds the Tabernacle to the plans and gives a second set of commandments.

Where Christianity has classically judged the God of the Old Testament to be a harsh God of Judgment, the rabbis understood that what the Torah was, in fact, what the history of Israel is, is the story of justice tempered with mercy. Yes, there were punishments (read: corrections), but there were always second chances. It is the story of *Adonai Elohim*.

## Yehudah ha-Levi Takes His Turn: Experience versus Cause

Yehudah ha-Levi was a Jewish poet and philosopher from the Golden Age of Spain. He wrote an important book of Jewish

---

[5]This image of "prototype people" is one I like a lot. I lifted it from Paul Johnson's *A History of the Jews* (New York: Harper & Row, 1987).

philosophy called *The Book of the Kuzari*, the story of a pagan king who converted to Judaism because of its beauty. In many ways, ha-Levi speaks to intersections and conflicts between Greek philosophy, particularly Aristotle, and rabbinic Judaism. It is his version of the problem of modernity. When he comes to speak of the difference between *Adonai* and *Elohim*, these issues come to the surface. This passage is found in *The Kuzari* 4:16:

> Now I understand the difference between *Adonai* and *Elohim*, and I can see that the God of Abraham is very different from that of Aristotle.

> People are drawn to *Adonai* out of love, reason, and conviction, while *Elohim* is compelling as the result of logic.

> Religious experiences lead people to give their lives for *Adonai* and to die for *Adonai*'s will. Reasoning, however, makes veneration only a necessity as long as it entails no harm, and as long as no pain results from it.

While I trust that both Socrates and Galileo would argue with ha-Levi's indictment of logic's lack of passionate commitment, the categories he presents are interesting and relevant.

> As we have stated in the beginning, *Adonai* is the God of Jewish history, The One-Who-Has-Evolved-a-Relationship-to-a-Particular-People through a set of shared experiences and commitments. The Merciful-One, The Torah-Giver, The Purveyor-of-Second-Chances is very much the personal, approachable God—The God-of-Religious Experiences, the God of Abraham.

> Likewise, *Elohim*, The Creator, The Absolute Judge, is The One-Who-Is-Accessible-to-All-People through a logical examination of the artifacts of creation. In order words, the order in the creation can reveal the order of The Creator. This is the God Whom the Jewish people share with Aristotle, and all those who seek the truth.

# A Collation

The two God names, *Adonai* and *Elohim*, reflect a series of dualities of religious possibility:[6]

1. *Adonai* = *Elohim*'s name      *Elohim* = *Adonai*'s role

2. *Adonai* = Mercy      *Elohim* = Justice

3. *Adonai* = The Revealer      *Elohim* = The Creator

4. *Adonai* = God of Jewish history   *Elohim* = Universal God

5. *Adonai* = God of Experience   *Elohim* = God of Logic

## The Grammar of Relationship

This duality of relationship is further suggested in the unusual grammar of the *brakhah* formula. Look carefully at the use of "person."

**a.**

בָּרוּךְ אַתָּה יהוה
*Barukh Atah Adonai*
Praised/Blessed are You, *Adonai*

---

[6]Do not think that this use of "duality" in any way undermines the unity of the One God. Just the opposite—it affirms it. In a wonderful passage about Hanukkah, Rabbi Nahman of Bratzlav teaches that the *dreidl* is the perfect symbol for the holiday, because it shows how Jewish logic defeated Greek logic. He explains, the Greeks could not understand that God could both be equally everywhere in the universe and uniquely found in the Temple in Jerusalem. For them, this defied "logic." The Jews, of course, saw reality as being like the *dreidl* with many sides of the truth, and saw this contradiction as part of the logic that makes *Adonai* God (*Sihot ha-Ran* 40).

## b.

### אֱלֹהֵינוּ מֶלֶךְ הָעוֹלָם
*Eloheinu Melekh ha-Olam*

our God, The Ruler-of-the-Cosmos . . . .

## c.

### אֲשֶׁר קִדְּשָׁנוּ בְּמִצְוֹתָיו וְצִוָּנוּ
*asher kidshanu b'mitzvotav, v'tzivanu*

The One-Who-Makes-Us-Holy with His *mitzvot*, and made it a *mitzvah* for us . . . .

The first portion (a) of our formula (*Barukh* + *Shem*) is clearly in the second person. God is a "You," and therefore seems close. In the last part, (c) (the *mitzvah* insertion[7]) God is clearly addressed in the third person. Here, God is "He." While part (b) the *Malkhut* is neutral (and could go with either grammatical form), because of what we have already learned about the connotations of *Elohim* as judge, the *Malkhut* is usually considered part of the third-person half of the *brakhah*.

This, like many other nuances we have isolated through close reading, evokes a question: Why does the *brakhah* formula change tense, jumping from second to third person in the middle?

There are a number of diverse rabbinic solutions available. Many solutions to this particular question draw on the metaphor of God as Ruler, not an unusual choice since it involves the *Malkhut*, the portion of the formula that describes God's Rulership. Perhaps the clearest of these comes from *Mahzor Vitry*. *Mahzor Vitry* is a collection of legal explanations of the laws of Jewish worship and celebration that was written and/or

---

[7]It is obvious that the *mitzvah*-insertion is not found in every *brakhah*. In fact, the ending of every *brakhah* is in the third person, speaking of God as a "The," being "The One-Who . . . ." Here the *mitzvah* insertion only serves as a relevant and clear example.

collected by Rabbi Simhah ben Samuel of Vitry, one of Rashi's
students (or perhaps one of his colleagues).

Here is the explanation found there.

> The first part of this formula is said as if one were speaking to a
> King mouth to mouth. Yet in the middle of the *brakhah*, we
> speak as if to an intermediary.
>
> [Compare "Blessed are You" to please tell the King that . . . "He
> is Our God, The Ruler-of-the-Cosmos. . . . "]
>
> Now here is the reason. David said (Psalm 16:8): "I have set
> *Adonai* Before me always. . . ."
>
> [This verse suggests that we can talk directly to God, because
> *Adonai* is before us.]
>
> In another place (Ezekiel 3:12) the Bible says: "Blessed be the
> Honor of God from His place."
>
> [This verse teaches that we cannot come close to God, because
> no one knows where "His Place" is.]
>
> How can we reconcile the two verses? When one is directly
> addressing God *Barukh Atah Adonai*, it is as David describes;
> God is before us and we can say "You," speaking with God
> mouth to mouth. But, when we are blessing God's Honor,
> *Eloheinu Melekh ha-Olam*, it is as Ezekiel describes, and we must
> bless God through a messenger.

Much is going on here. But beneath the textual richness and
midrashic play is the same basic twofold human experience of
the Divine we found in use of God's two names.

Simply put, there are times in our lives when God is an easy
and obvious experience, when saying "You" is natural and
comfortable. Often, these are moments of love, family, closeness, and success. At these times we feel privileged and
perhaps a little special. There are other times where God, if in

existence, is clearly remote and abstract. These are often times of fear, frustration, doubt—perhaps moments of failure—certainly moments of uncertainty. It is then that we speak of God (or if we dare, to God) more haltingly; the word *If* begins to come up a lot. Here, the privilege of saying "You" is long forgotten, and we "hope" (yes, and pray) that our message will get through.

## The Experience of Relationship

My friend and teacher, Rabbi Lawrence Kushner, relays the same insight in another way. He tells this story.[8]

Once I was to lead a Shabbos afternoon discussion with some grade school children from the congregation. I wanted to talk with them about holy matters and so I asked them if they believed in God. I thought that some would and some wouldn't and that we would have a lively discussion. But to my astonishment, no one raised a hand. They were not spiteful or disinterested or even impious. As a matter of fact, they were serious, interested, and honest. And by their silence they were simply saying that they did not believe in God. In much the same way they might have said matter of factly that it wasn't raining . . . .

And then some time later on (during that same unremembered discussion) I thought of a different question. Or maybe it was the same question. I asked them if any of them had ever been close to God. And everyone of them raised their hands. Freely and naturally. Unaware of any contradiction or inconsistency. But now I had to have proof, so I asked them when and where. And one by one they described what I believe to be, the Jewish experience of God. One told of the previous evening when we had lit the Shabbos candles. Another of a few months ago amidst anger and sadness upon the death of grandparent. And still another of a few days earlier when even though they didn't feel like it, they helped one of their parents.

---

[8]Lawrence Kushner, *Honey From the Rock* (San Francisco: Harper & Row, 1977), pp. 16–17.

*Adonai* is the Jewish experience of feeling close. It is the name
we give the part of the God experience that transcends logic
and belief, that instead has to do with family and closeness.
*Adonai* is the God experience of the Exodus and of the *Shabbat*
candles, of Abraham's hospitality and of *seder* at our grandpar-
ents. *Adonai* is the God found in our memories, national,
familiar, and even personal. It is the inner, private God feeling,
the one that doesn't need explanation or justification—the one
we know rather than understand.

Jewish worship begins with saying the Name: *Adonai*. It asks
us to root our worship experience in its sublogical truth. Like
the slight shiver of the tactile residue of a well-remembered hug
or the half-hummable inner echo of lullabies that carried us off
to sleep in a distant childhood, the name *Adonai* provides us
with our own safe start toward the holy.

As Jews, it is our family privilege, one paid for by the
dedication of generations of Covenant Keepers, to speak to
God mouth to mouth—at least for an instant. After all, we have
the phone number—our Mother gave it to us.

# 6

# Rumpelstiltskin and Blessing

The function of the *Shem*—Part 2: The use of God's Name—*Adonai*—is a radical affirmation of the populous grounding of the rabbinic Jewish worship. It empowers everyone.

## A Rabbinic Revolution

### The Oral Torah = Continuously Rewritten History

According to the rabbis themselves (and *Pirke Avot* 1:1 is a good starting point), rabbinic Judaism is nothing more than the linear continuation of the original revelation of the Torah, the one Moses received on Mount Sinai. In their version of those forty days and forty nights, God revealed two Torahs at the same time:

1. A Written Law, *Torah she-be-Ktav*, which is the document, the Torah

2. An Oral Law, *Torah she-be-al Peh*, which is the progressive
   interpretation of the written document.

Here is the way they describe the transmission of the insight
and the authority of Torah:

> **Moses** received the Torah on Mt. Sinai
> and transmitted it to **Joshua**,
> **Joshua** transmitted it to the **Elders**,
> The **Elders** transmitted it to the **Prophets**,
> and the **Prophets** transmitted it to the **Men of the Great
> Assembly.**

The Men of the Great Assembly were the sages, the prototype
rabbis, and through them, with their monopoly on authentic
interpretation via the Oral Law, the culmination of the Torah
process occurs.

Oral Law was a brilliant innovation that allowed for a continual, progressive rewriting of history. It said, in essence, that
everything we teach was once taught in the original lesson—
every innovation we make is nothing more than the completion
of God's original intent. Claiming that progressive revelation is
limited to a specific chain of transmission is a great way to
rewrite history. As long as it works, one continues to never
lose.

If you look carefully at this passage from *Pirke Avot*, you will
notice that the *kohanim* have been left out of the loop. This is
more than an oversight. It was the *kohanim* who were the
original guardians of the Ark and the Torah. They should be at
the core of its transmission. In a real sense, the ball is instead
passed on (or better, "lateraled") to the elders (a neodemocratic
group) and then handed off to the prophets (the official
adversaries of the formal religious cult). In rewriting history,
the rabbis dealt with the priesthood in four ways.

1. The rabbis proscribed the power of the Temple, leaving the
   priesthood, its power, and its role out of what they defined

as the central thrust of Jewish life, the Torah and its transmission.

2. Before the destruction of the Temple, the rabbis worked hard to limit the priesthood's power by granting the Sanhedrin (a body they controlled) the right to use *halakhah* (the legal process they controlled) to prescribe the precise procedures for Temple rituals.

3. After the destruction of the Temple, the rabbis made a point of carefully recording and preserving the rituals and symbolic centrality of the Temple and its practices in a kind of intellectual formaldehyde, making sure that no renewed life was possible.

4. The rabbis slowly undermined the Temple's religious centrality by creating a system of holy encounters that took place in the home, the synagogue, and the *Bet Midrash* (House of Study), thereby undercutting the actual influence of the priesthood on the average Jew's daily life.

In the end, however, the rabbis' deadly blow to the Temple's importance was achieved by increasing the aura that surrounded its performances, thereby limiting the cult's day-to-day power by making it a completely holy realm, wholly separate from the people. The Temple became a once- or twice-a-year experience, a Sukkot and Pesah equivalent of our own High Holiday Judaism. It existed in marked contrast to the daily areas of Jewish life, all of which the rabbis controlled. The priests, the original purveyors of Jewish religion, had been disenfranchised as power players; they now were merely the functionaries in a compelling but noninfluential public spectacle.

In truth, this revolution against the centrality of the Temple cult is critical to our understanding of the *brakhah* system and the development of the *brakhah* formula, because in a real sense, the *brakhah* was the prime weapon used to decentralize

Jewish worship. Later in this chapter, we will carefully trace the evolution of the power of God's name and, with it, a disenfranchisement of the priesthood.

## A Rabbinic History in Just over Sixty Seconds

To put this all into context, here is a very quick history of the formulation and evolution of rabbinic Judaism.

In 928 B.C.E., after Solomon's death, the Land of Israel was split into two Kingdoms: Israel (ten of the tribes) and Judah (Judah and little Benjamin) when Jeroboam led a break-away rebellion against Solomon's son, Rehoboam.

In 732, Tiglath-pileser III, the king of Assyria, conquered and destroyed Israel, leaving only Judah. The "Israelites" were carried away and vanished forever from Jewish history, leaving only Judah (and little Benjamin).

In the low 600s (B.C.E.) Assyria lost power. Its empire and the renewed Egyptian empire were slowly gobbled up by the new force on the scene, Babylonia. On the 9th of the month of *Av*, 586 B.C.E., Nebuchadnezzar conquered Jerusalem and Judah fell. However, Jeremiah, the leading prophet of this era, prophesied that Babylonia, too, would fall and that the Jewish people would return in 70 years.

Jeremiah was correct. In 439 B.C.E., Cyrus, the founding king of the Persian Empire, outmaneuvered Nabonius (Nebuchadnezzar's heir) and took control of the Babylonian Empire, making it his own. One of his first actions was to give the Jews permission to return. In 438 B.C.E. a Jewish leader known as Ezra the Scribe led the Jewish people back to Israel and began the process of rebuilding both the Temple and the nation. This began the era of the Second Temple.

Ezra began the process of reforming Judaism. In the Talmud, *Bava Kamma* 82a, we are given a list.

Ten Fixes That Ezra fixed:[1]

1. That the Torah be read publically at Shabbat *Minhah* Services

2. That the Torah be read publically on Mondays and Thursdays

3. That courts be held on Mondays and Thurdays

4. That clothes be washed on Thursdays[2]

5. That garlic be eaten on Fridays[3]

6. That the housewife rise early to bake bread[4]

---

[1]This *baraita* will break into three sets of innovations with some additional confusion. First, there is a reformation of worship, taking the reading of Torah and the presence of courts and making them a local, neighborhood affair rather than a national process. Second, the home (rather than Temple) observance of *Shabbat* is given some prominence. Third, laws of family purity, modesty, and ritual cleanliness of women are underscored. All three of these are classic rabbinic foci. The nonsequiturs are "the spice rule" that the Talmud equates with women buying eye make-up in order to be beautiful in her husband's eyes (but may have more to do with economic reform) and the early morning bread baking, which is discussed in a footnote below.

[2]This is to insure the celebration of *Shabbat*. Clean clothes were a practical start.

[3]The *Gemara* gives a great explanation of this one: "Rabbi Judah, or perhaps Rabbi Nahman, or perhaps Rabbi Kahana, or even perhaps Rabbi Yohanan stated that this refers to a man fulfilling his marital duty every Friday night." Garlic, after all, is an aphrodesiac. My question about this *baraita*, however, is the reason behind the doubted authorship. Did no one want to take credit, or did every one?

[4]The *Gemara* suggests that "a woman rise early to bake bread—so that there should be bread for the poor."

7. That a woman must wear a *sinnar*[5]

8. That a woman must comb her hair before going to the *mikvah*

9. That spice sellers be allowed to travel between the towns

10. That a person who has a "pollution" must go to the *mikvah*.

Ezra's reforms change Jewish life. Most significant, but not readily visible to us, is the revolutionary nature of the first two of these "fixes," which declare the public reading of Torah (in the synagogue). Previously, the Torah had belonged to the priests and public readings were limited to the small sections they chose to use liturgically. What had once been the "secret knowledge" of the cult was now thrown open to the whole people. In many, many ways, rabbinic Judaism gets its start from this single act.

It would be nice to say that the Temple was the central force in Jewish life and that the synagogue was invented in Babylonia as a way of coping with its destruction, but archeology has shown that isn't true. Even though *The New Jewish History* I studied in fifth grade Hebrew school taught that as a definitive truth, it is clear that synagogues were evolving before the Babylonian exile. It is probably that they grew in importance there, and thereby influenced Ezra's reforms.

In the mid 300s B.C.E., Alexander the Great conquered most of the known world, including Judea (332 B.C.E.) (soon to be Palestina). This brought about great economic changes, including the growth of the city and the rise of a middle (merchant) class. In the cities two political-religious-social parties/groups evolved: Hellenizers, who wanted more assimilation into Greek culture (and included many of the old, rich, priestly families), and *hasidim*, who were after a more intensive

---

[5]The meaning of *sinnar* is obscure (some say "underwear," others say "a girdle," and so on), though the connotation is as the *Gemara* suggests, "out of modesty."

religious renewal. (The *hasidim* were by and large made up of former farmers who were part of the new urban middle class.) They centered much of their life around the newly evolving synagogues.

The Hanukkah War was in 164 B.C.E. In reality it was a civil war between *hasidim* and Hellenizers that was exacerbated by a slightly mad Syrian despot, Antiochus III, and became a revolution. In its wake, temporary religious freedom was won. However, the real victory is that of the *hasidim*, who gained control over the Temple and its practices, as well as the Sanhedrin, the national religious decision-making body. We can't say for sure that Ezra's students become the *hasidim*, but they clearly are his extension.

By 63 B.C.E., the positions have remained constant, but the names have changed. The foreign rulers were now the Romans. The assimilationists (including many from the rich priestly families) were a political party called the Sadduces, and the middle-class religious renewal group were called the Pharisees. Starting around 30 B.C.E., they began collecting their teachings and those of their ancestors and formalizing their position. This process of collection was completed around 200 C.E. and became the *Mishnah*. Rabbinic Judaism is Pharisaic Judaism.

In 70 C.E., the Temple was destroyed, Jerusalem was destroyed, and the center of Jewish life shifted. It first went to Yavneh, a small city with a rabbinic academy, located essentially where Ben Gurion Airport stands today. Here, under Rabban Yohanan ben Zakkai, the Jews began a process of reconstructing Judaism without a Temple or a king—rabbinic Judaism was now fully in power.

In 132 C.E., under the leadership of Bar Kokhba, and backed by the religious authority of Rabbi Akiva and others, the Jews successfully rebelled against Rome and won a short period of freedom. By 135, the revolt had ended, new pursections had begun, and Jewish life in Judea was all but over.

By 210, Judah the Prince, the head of the Sanhedrin, completed the redaction of the *Mishnah* in the Galilee, and the focus of Jewish life shifted to Babylonia. There the talmudic

academies flourished for another 300 years, culminating in the
completion of the *Gemara*.

## Yohanan ben Zakkai as Revolutionary

In many ways, Rabban Yohanan ben Zakkai was the
founding hero of rabbinic Judaism. While several generations
had nurtured its ideology and practices and had developed its
regiments and influences, it was Rabban Yohanan ben Zakkai
who singlehandedly gave it its full life. If Ezra the Scribe was
the progenitor of the rabbinic spirit, it was Yohanan ben Zakkai
who brought it to fullfillment.

In *Avot D'Rabbi Natan* (a midrashic commentary on *Pirke Avot*)
we find this version of the legend. Jerusalem was besieged by
the Romans. Inside, the Jews were fighting among themselves,
too. The Zealots were a group of religious radicals, a "Give me
liberty or give me death" sect who killed anyone who talked
"surrender or compromise" by throwing them over the city
wall. Our hero, Yohanan ben Zakkai, a promient Pharisee and
an active member of the "Peace Party," has it announced that
he is dead. He is then sewn into a shroud with a couple of dead
cats and carried outside the city for burial by his students. Once
outside, he goes straight to Vespasian, the Roman general and
says, "Howdy, Caesar."

Vespasian shakes his head and says, "I am a general, not a
Caeser."

Yohanan ben Zakkai says, "But you soon will be," and he
cites a couple of verses from the prophet Isaiah to prove it. (The
essence is: Jerusalem can only fall to a king. You're going to
take Jerusalem. Ergo, you will be Caesar.) Just as Yohanan ben
Zakkai finishes speaking, the messenger from Rome arrives
with "the news"; Vespasian mentally dons his laurel wreath
and asks Yohanan ben Zakkai, "What do you want?"

Yohanan responds humbly, "Just give me Yavneh and her
scholars."

Jerusalem was destroyed. Masada held out for three years
and then was destroyed. Meanwhile, Yohanan ben Zakkai and

his band of merry Pharisees are in Yavneh, happily redefining Judaism and evolving a Temple-free rabbinic Judaism. Here's an excerpt of the process (*Rosh ha-Shanah* 29b):

## Mishnah

If Rosh ha-Shanah fell on *Shabbat*,
They used to blow the *shofar* in the Temple, but not elsewhere.
After the destruction of the Temple, Rabban Yohanan ben Zakkai ruled:
It should be blown every place where there is a *Bet Din* (a rabbinical court).

Rabbi Eleazar said:
You've got it wrong—
Rabban Yohanan ben Zakkai made this ruling only for Yavneh.
The Majority said to Him:
[No, You've got it wrong—]
The ruling applies equally to Yavneh
and any other place with a *Bet Din*. . . .

## Gemara

Our Rabbis taught:
Once Rosh ha-Shanah fell on *Shabbat*.
Rabban Yohanan ben Zakkai said to some of those who disagreed with him:
"Let's blow the *shofar* [here in Yavneh]."
They said to him:
"Let's discuss the matter. [Is it correct to blow the *shofar* on *Shabbat* here?]"
He said to them:
"Let's blow it now and discuss it later."

After the *shofar* was sounded, they said to him:
"Now, let's discuss the question."
He answered:
"The *shofar* has already been sounded in Yavneh; what has already been done is no longer open to discussion."

In this passage, we get a sense, not only of the personality
and political skill of Yohanan ben Zakkai, but of the way
rabbinic authority decentralized the Temple experience, putting their own process in its place. We'll now see the same
thing happen with the *brakhah* formula's use of *Adonai*.

## The Evolution of the Power of the Name

### One Name, Two Fences

The rabbis were both conservative and conservational in
their revolution. While radically remodeling the Jewish tradition, they were also involved themselves in finding ways of
providing structural stability. One of their key structural innovations was a concept called *Siyag le-Torah*, putting a fence
around the Torah. It worked like this.

> The Torah tells us not to work on *Shabbat*. It is a very important
> *mitzvah*. We don't want anyone to violate this *mitzvah*, so we'll
> protect it. We'll put a fence around it. We will add our own law
> that says that no one is allowed to touch a tool on *Shabbat*. If you
> can't touch a tool, you can't work. The tool rule will make it
> much harder to forget about *Shabbat* and do just a little work by
> mistake. The tool rule is a fence around *Shabbat*, protecting the
> "don't work" *mitzvah*.

The two "fences" constructed around God's name, one
having to do with pronouncing it and the other having to do
with writing it, are both rabbinic in origin, although they can be
construed as expressions of the third commandment, "You
shall not take the name of *Adonai*, Your God, in vain."

### Fence 1: *Kiddushin* 71a

In a discussion of power of specific legal degrees, the rabbis go
off on a tangent, the power and magic in God's name. In the
midst of that discussion we find this rule, which "fences" the
pronunciation of the Tetragrammaton.

Narrator: Rabbi Abina [taught a lesson] by connecting [the] two [parts of that] verse:

Rabbi
Abinia: [In Exodus 3:15] God says:

Torah: This is My name:

Rabbi
Abina: [And later in that verse God says:]

Torah: This is My Memorial.

Rabbi
Abina: The Holy-One-Who-Is-to-Be-Blessed [put these two phrases together] to say, "I am not to be called [memorialized] the same way I am written (My Name). My name is to be written יה, but it is to be pronounced אד (Adonai).

## Fence 2: *Shevuot* 35a

In the tractate devoted to oaths, the rabbis discuss the kinds of legal formulae that are binding. In the midst of this they turn to a discussion of swearing by (and against) God's name. In the process, they discuss writing God's name. Here is what they say.

There are Names [of God] that may be erased
and there are names [of God] that may not be erased.

## List A

These are the Names that may not be erased:
אֵל (El), [which means "God"],
אֱלֹהַּ (Eloha), [a variation of El],
אֱלֹהִים (Elohim), [another variation of El],
אֱלֹהֶיךָ (Elohekha), [another variation meaning "Your God"],
אֶהְיֶה אֲשֶׁר אֶהְיֶה (Ehiyeh asher Ehiyeh), [which means "I am that I am"],
אד, [the two letters that stand for "Adonai"]

יה, [the two letters that stand for the Tetragrammaton],
שַׁדַּי (Shaddai), [which means "God on High"], and
צְבָאוֹת (Tzeva'ot), [which means "Hosts"].

## List B

But
הַגָּדוֹל (ha-Gadol), [which means "The Great"],
הַגִּבּוֹר (ha-Gibor), [which means "The Mighty"],
הַנּוֹרָא (ha-Norah), [which means "The Awesome"],
הָאַדִּיר (ha-Adir), [which means "The Loved"],
הֶחָזָק (ha-Hazak), [which means "The Strong"],
הָאַמִּיץ (ha-Amitz), [which means "The Powerful"],
הָעִזּוּז (ha-Uzuz), [which means "The Forceful"],
חַנּוּן וְרַחוּם (Hanun V'Rahun), [which means "The Kind-and-The-
    Merciful"],
אֶרֶךְ אַפַּיִם (Erekh Apim), [which means "The Long-Suffering"], and
וְרַב חֶסֶד (v'Rav Hesed), [which means "The One-Who-is-Great-
    with-Kindness"]—
These may be erased.

All the names on both lists are biblical. List A, those that cannot
be erased (and therefore should only be written as a last resort),
are actual names of God. List B, those that may be erased (and
therefore can be written anywhere), are descriptions of God
and have functions outside of God's name. Therefore, the basic
principle of this second fence is that any letters that are
specifically and exclusively God's name should only be written
with special care and only in very limited circumstances,
because they can never be erased. The reasoning here seems
obvious: God's name should not be taken, spoken, or written
in vain.

## A Problem *Baraita*

This same idea of being careful with God's name (in print) is
also expressed in a story found in another talmudic passage,
*Rosh ha-Shanah* 18a. However, this time the Talmud raises some

serious questions. To help you understand this passage, here are two clues.

Clue 1: Greeks = Antiochus

Clue 2: Hasmoneans = Maccabees

Now for our story:

On the third of [the Hebrew Month] of *Tishre* the mention [of God's Name] in legal bonds was abolished.

The Greek government had forbidden the mention of God's name by the Families of Israel, and so, when the kingdom of the Hasmoneans became strong and defeated them, they started a practice of mentioning God's name, even on bonds.

They used to write them like this: "In the year, so-and-so of Yohanan, High Priest to the *El Elyon*, God Most High . . . .

But when the sages heard about this, they said, "Tomorrow this person will pay his debt and the bond [with God's name] will be thrown on a dunghill." The sages stopped this practice.

This small sound-bite of rabbinic history clearly echoes the sentiment that God's name is to be protected, but it also does something else—it shows us that meanings and understandings change.

a. If it hadn't been a common practice to use God's name in an oral or written form, then Antiochus wouldn't have banned its use (and no one would have cared).

b. If it had been a clear biblical prohibition not to write down God's name, Yohanan would never have done it.

Rather, this special protection of God's name is clearly a rabbinic innovation. What we see here is the Oral Law in action.

## A Biblical Spectacle

And now for a desert spectacular.

Imagine that we are in the midst of the Book of Leviticus, standing outside the Tent of Meeting—part of the desert sequence. The whole Jewish people has been assembled. It is Yom Kippur, the holiest day of the Jewish year. The celebration has been going on since last night. Everyone is fasting. Everyone is hungry. Everyone is hot, and tired, and excited, and involved.

The people are gathered inside and out the Tent of Meeting. Inside the Tent of Meeting, the Altar with its Ever-Burning Light is standing. Many Levites and *Kohanim* are going about their duties. At the center there is a smaller tent, the Tabernacle, covered in many layers of skins. Inside, if we could see in, are two rooms: the Holy, and the Holy of Holies. In the Holy the *menorah*, the table for the shew bread, the laver, and the other sacred items are kept. Inside the Holy of Holies, the Ark of the Covenant stands.

This is not just any Yom Kippur. Tragedy has recently struck. Nadav and Avihu, two of Aaron's sons, had improvised their own creative worship experiences. They had "brought a strange fire before *Adonai*" and somehow had died in the process. To make sure that no such accident would ever occur again, God gives Aaron a precise set of fixed procedures— every step is exactly defined. This Yom Kippur is when they will first be used. Here is where we pick up the Torah's narration starting at Leviticus 16:6. Here, God warns Moses:

"Tell your brother Aaron that he cannot come into the Holy at any time he chooses. He should not go behind 'the Curtain,' which is the cover over the Ark of the Covenant [in the Holy of Holies] for I appear in the cloud over the cover."

Then, as the narration continues, God gives Moses a precise outline of the steps Aaron is to follow to prepare himself to enter the Holy of Holies. Once he is ready, this is the plan.

Aaron should take the two he-goats and let them stand before *Adonai* at the entrance of the Tent of Meeting. He shall cast lots between the two goats and mark one for *Adonai* and the other for *Azazel*. Aaron shall then take the goat marked for *Adonai* and offer it as a sin offering, while the goat marked for *Azazel* shall be left standing, alive, before the *Adonai*, to make atonement through it, and to send it off to the wilderness for *Azazel*.

At this point, Aaron is to offer his bull as a sin offering for himself and his family. He is to slaughter his bull as a sin offering and then take a panful of glowing coals scooped from the altar before *Adonai*, add two handfuls of finely ground incense, and place this behind "the Curtain" [to the Holy of Holies]. He shall put the incense on the fire before *Adonai*, so that the cloud of smoke from the incense serves as a screen, hiding the Ark of the Covenant, lest he die. . . . When he goes in to make atonement in the Tabernacle, nobody else shall be in the Tent of Meeting until he comes out. . . .

What follows is an elaborate series of sacrifices and ritual cleansings using the blood from the sacrifices. With everything "clean" and "pure," we are ready to move on to the next step of the ritual.

When he has finished purging the Tabernacle, the Tent of Meeting, and the altar, the live goat is brought forward. Aaron shall lay both his hands upon the head of the live goat and confess over it all the missed marks and transgressions of the Families of Israel, putting them on the head of the goat, and it shall be sent off to the wilderness . . . thus the goat shall carry on him all their sins to an inaccessible region. . . .

This passage is biblical worship at its best—spectacle with substance. While there is much that we can examine, two concepts are central. First is the clear notion that God is present. When Jews pray, God is there—right there. Second, the big concern in this text is "not seeing God." While the mystics debate the transcendent power of a God image, and while science fiction types try to turn the smoke-filled Tabernacle into an ancient Middle Eastern version of the Wizard of Oz's mechanical voting booth, the clear religious experience here involves proximity.

## A Postbiblical Spectacle

By the time of the *Mishnah*, the Tabernacle was long gone. David had brought it to Jerusalem and Solomon, David's son, had reconstructed it as a huge Temple (also with courtyards, a Holy, and a Holy of Holies). Solomon's Temple was destroyed and then rebuilt, and the Ark of the Covenant and all the other original holy artifacts have been lost. To keep us in historical context, the real work on the *Mishnah* begins shortly after the Hannukah story, in the turmoil between the Syrian and Roman conquests of Judea.

In the *Mishnah*, in the section of the order on seasonal celebrations, *Moed*, in the book on Yom Kippur, *Yoma*, we have a detailed description of the Temple ritual. In Chapter 6, *Mishnah* 2, the High Priest, the *Kohein ha-Gadol*, the one who has inherited Aaron's job, puts his hands on the scapegoat, the goat for *Azazel*. In the thousand years since we last watched this ritual, much has changed.

Next he came to the Scapegoat and placed his two hands [between the horns] and confessed. This is what he said:

"I pray, **The Name**

Your People, the House of Israel, have done wrong, they have missed-the-mark, they have transgressed before You.

I pray [with] **The Name**

Please forgive the iniquities, the transgressions, and the missed-marks that Your People, the House of Israel have errored before You."

Each time the High Priest says the *ha-Shem*, **the Name**, there is great anticipation. For everyone knows what will follow.

As it is written in the Torah of Moses, Your servant (Leviticus 16:30): "For on this day will atonement be made for you, to make you clean from all your missed-marks. Before יהוה you shall become clean."

At this point, for the one and only time in the year, the *Kohein ha-Gadol* says out loud the secret, not-otherwise-uttered real pronounciation of יהוה. There is a tremendous reaction.

And when the *Kohanim* who were standing in the courtyard heard יהוה, **"The Unspoken Name,"** pronounced from the *Kohein ha-Gadol*'s mouth, they went down, knelt, fell on their faces, and said:

בָּרוּךְ שֵׁם כְּבוֹד מַלְכוּתוֹ לְעוֹלָם וָעֶד
*Barukh Shem Kevod Malkhuto le-Olam va-Ed*

*Barukh* be **the Name** Whose Honored Kingdom is for eternity and more.

While there was more to follow, this was it, the *denouement*, the moment—the one time God's true name was said out loud. The High Priest had assured their forgiveness by using their most powerful national tool, the direct access code to God's will.

The big shift between the biblical and mishnaic descriptions of Yom Kippur is clearly the role of "the Name." Just as in the story of Yohanan, God's name is now of central importance. Whereas in the Bible, the proximity of God and the *Kohein ha-Gadol*'s ability to enter the Holy of Holies and get close is the key factor, here it is the use of the "Secret Name." By mishnaic times, the "Name," more than the location has become the way to influence God. What we are watching is a kind of Rumpel-stiltskin-like mysticism.

## Rumpelstiltskin and Prayer

| | |
|---|---|
| Princess: | Is it Ichabod? |
| Rumpelstiltskin: | No! (*He smiles*) |
| Princess: | Is it Edward? |
| Rumpelstiltskin: | No! (*He laughs*) |
| Princess: | Is it Rumpelstiltskin? |
| Rumpelstiltskin: | Ahhhhhhhh . . . hhhh . . . ! (*He screams and runs away.*) |

The folk story Rumpelstiltskin reflects an ancient piece of conventional wisdom: knowing someone's name gives you power over them. Jews have long seen names as a source of power and control.

God gives Adam the right to name the animals, and the names he chooses influences their nature.

God changes Abram and Sarai's names as part of the covenant.

God changes Jacob's name as symbol of transformation.

Moses changes Hoshea into Joshua as a sign of power.

In our own way, too, we understand that names have power. I have a friend named "Thorten." He calls himself "Rocky." He always has. He doesn't want anyone to know his real name. He's afraid that anyone who knew his real name would have the power to pick on him.

My mother also knows the secret of a name's power. She uses my full real name, "Joel Lurie Grishaver," every time she wants to yell at me. Likewise, many of my close friends call me "Gris," a nickname, as a way of capturing my attention. Only David Meyer is different. He has been a friend for almost twenty years. He calls me "Haver." That is his special way of making me focus.

When I was growing up, the Tilson family had the apartment upstairs. Mrs. Tilson also knew that names had power. Every morning she would remind her sons Newt (who was really Hugh, Jr.) and Max (whose real name I can't recall), "Have a good day, and never forget that your name is Tilson."

I'm sure you can add your own "name-wisdom." A name is sometimes called a "handle." That is because a name is a way of grabbing someone's attention. It is something that has a hold on you. When you hear your name, you stop and listen. That is a name's special power. Special names (like nicknames) have special power because they carry context. And it was, and still is, believed that knowing the right way to address God maximizes the chance that your prayers will be heard.[6]

Even though any sensitivity to "the Name" seems absent in the Bible's Yom Kippur, that is the central principle at work in the use of "the Name" in our *Mishnah*. This becomes even more clear when we progress ahead another five hundred years or so.

## A Talmudic Reflection

In this dialogue, *Kiddushin* 71a, preserved from some study session in the Babylonia academy, we hear a talmudic re-working of the insights in the *Mishnah*.

---

[6]Practical mysticism is essentially "religious magic." Knowing God's secret names has long been the essence of Jewish practical mysticism. The Baal Shem Tov, the Master of the Good Name (or better translated as "the Good Master of the Name"), the founder of hasidic Judaism, was one of a long line of Name Masters who were reputed to use their secret knowledge of God's name to do good.

a.

Rabbah
ben Bar
Hanah:        Rabbi Yohanan said:

Rabbi
Yohanan:      The sages only taught the pronunciation of the
              Tetragrammaton to their disciples once in a
              cycle of seven.

Narrator:     Others say they taught its pronunciation twice
              a cycle of seven.[7]

Rabbi
Nahman
ben Isaac:    Logic suggests that it was [no more often] than
              once in a cycle of seven because it says [in
              Exodus 3:15]:

Torah:        זֶה־שְׁמִי לְעֹלָם
              This is My Eternal Name [le-Olam].

Rabbi
Nahman
ben Isaac:    [But] in the Torah, [the word] לְעוֹלָם is written
              [without the letter וֹ, making it] לְעַלֵּם [which
              means "to be kept secret]."

              Raba was once planning to give a public lecture
              on this topic, but a certain old man said to him:

Old Man:      It is written in the Torah: לְעַלֵּם—to be kept
              secret.

Rabbi
Nahman
ben Isaac:    Raba then canceled the lecture.

---

[7]The Hebrew for "cycle of seven" is *shavua*, which normally means
"week." Here, however, the context seems to rule that out. Most
probably, we are now talking about a seven-year cycle, made prom-
inent by the Sabbatical year (the seventh year, when the land rested).

In the Bible, יהוה seems to be commonplace. It is spoken out loud with no apparent hesitation.[8] Likewise, in the biblical Yom Kippur we observed, the saying of the Name seemed to be of no great importance—it isn't in any way highlighted or referenced in the biblical text's description of the procedure. In the *Mishnah*, however, an earlier rabbinic layer, the Name was now an important and powerful tool that seemed to be entrusted to the priesthood. In this passage, we see that the Name has remained powerful, become secret, and become entrusted to the rabbis. To own the power of the Name, you now need to be a student of rabbinic Judaism, not a descendant of Aaron.

---

[8]We are dealing here with an argument from silence. This is always an intellectual problem. By showing a pattern of systematic introduction, I am suggesting that certain ideas are being grown within the Jewish tradition. Here, specifically, I am suggesting that this "Name-as-power" focus on the Tetragrammaton is something that was not from Torah (where the big issue seems to be seeing God) and was added in later periods, evolving into a major issue in rabbinic times. I do this because of the absence of earlier mentions. It is possible, however, and this is how a Torah-true Oral Law supporter would argue, that the rabbinic issues were consistantly part of the Oral interpretation and understanding of the text, and only came to be written down later in the process, where there was a fear that they would be lost. As it usually is, given Jewish parameters, Torah is what you believe it to be.

The specific problem to my thesis is Leviticus 24:15 ff. There it says, "Whosoever curses God will have sinned. And one who *v'ney-kov v'ney-kov*'s יהוה name shall surely be put to death." Some sources understand the verb in this second verse to be "profane"; others suggest that it means "pronounce outloud." The latter is the reading of the *Targum*, an Aramaic translation from the second century. Rashi follows the latter, but again, this is a late reading. If, however, you examine the text in terms of poetic parallelism, the word that these latter sources understand as "pronounce" (which I believe must constitute isogesis, a reading into the text's meaning) has to be a parallel to "curses," suggesting a negative utterance, not a mere pronunciation.

Note: The Raba story at the end also suggests that the secret-
ness of the Name is an emerging phenomenon. Otherwise,
Raba would have never considered giving the lecture in the
first place.

b.

Narrator:   Rabbi Abina [taught a lesson] by connecting
            the two [parts of that] verse:

Rabbi
Abina:      [In Exodus 3:15] God says:

Torah:      This is my name:

Rabbi
Abina:      [And later in that verse God says]:

Torah:      This is My Memorial.

Rabbi
Abina:      The Holy-One-Who-Is-to-Be-Blessed [put these
            two phrases together] to say, "I am not to be
            called (memorialized) the same way I am writ-
            ten (My Name). My name is to be written יה, but
            it is to be pronounced Adonai.

This passage is one we examined earlier. It uses classic rabbinic
midrashic exegesis to explain a difference. Because God has a
"Name," and a way of being "memorialized," the rabbis
suggest that the "Name" is to be kept private and unspoken,
and the "memorial" is to be publicized and used everywhere.
Ultimately, the Shem potion of the brakhah formula will use the
"memorial."

c.

Narrator:   Our rabbis taught:

Baraita:    At first all of the people [of Israel] were trusted with the twelve-letter Name [of God]. Then, when many of them grew to be unfit, its [knowledge] was limited to the pious *kohanim*, and they [made it a practice] to swallow its [pronunciation] when they said it [during the priestly benediction] with their brother priests.

Narrator:  It is taught:

Rabbi
Tarfon:  I once went up on the *bimah*, following my mother's brothers, and listened carefully to the *Kohein ha-Gadol*. I actually heard him swallow the Name during the chanting of his brother priests.

Don't ask about the twelve-letter name of God. I don't know it. Neither does anyone else. It is an echo of mystery religions that were popular at this time. It is, however, obviously an expansion of the Tetragrammaton. What is important here is the acknowledgment of a historical progression. First, every Jew could use God's name. Then just the priests. Then just the High Priests. The power of God's name was slowly becoming a secret.

d.

Rabbi
Judah:  Rav taught:

Rav:  The forty-two-letter name of God is only entrusted to a person who is pious, meek, middle-aged, free from bad temper, sober, not insistent on his rights. One who knows this name is careful of it and observes its purity, is popular above and popular below, is held in awe by people, and inherits two worlds: this world and the world to come.

What Rabbi Judah is making explicit here is that knowledge of "the Name," becoming a "Name Master," is an ethical issue, a question of right living, not of priestly birth. The final power, the final secret, now resides in a person who truly lives out the Torah (as expressed in the rabbinic way of life). The secret of the name now belongs to the rabbis. It has been appropriated.

## The Role of the Name in the *Brakhah* Formula: A Rereading

We have previously examined this portion of the *Gemara* (*Brakhot* 40b) in the second chapter of this book. There, we used it to understand the importance of formula in the standarization of Jewish practice. We're now going to reread it in the context of the rest of this chapter. This time, it is to be seen as an ideological, political statement.

| | |
|---|---|
| Rabbi Meir: | If a person sees a loaf of bread and says: |
| Person: | "What a fine loaf of bread this is! Bless *ha-Makom* Who Created it. |
| Rabbi Meir: | This person has fulfilled the *mitzvah*. . . . |
| Rabbi Yosi: | [I think you are wrong.] If a person changes the formula "minted" by the rabbis, that person has not fulfilled the obligation. . . . |
| Narrator: | Benjamin, the shepherd, made a sandwich, [ate it,] and then said in Aramaic: |
| Benjamin: | Blessed be The Master-of-this-Bread. |
| Narrator: | [Rav ruled]: |

Rav: He has fulfilled his obligation [to say a *brakhah* after eating].

Student: [How could] Rav [accept this as a *brakhah*?] Didn't he teach?

Rav: Any *brakhah* that doesn't mention God's name is not a real *brakhah*.

Narrator: Then we must guess that [we have remembered this event incorrectly. Benjamin] must have said [something like]:

Benjamin: Blessed be The All-Merciful, The Master-of-this-Bread.

With different considerations at work, the real debate between Rabbi Yosi and everyone else is the use of *Adonai*, not the presence of the *Malkhut*. Rav's opinion was that a *brakhah* must mention God's name, but the formula that is finally considered acceptable uses "a name that can be erased," really an attribute of God.

The core issue underneath this text seems to be a question of "fencing." Everyone agrees that a *brakhah* should indicate God to be The Source-of-All-Blessings, that is the purpose of the *Shem* part of the formula. Everyone is also in agreement that the יהוה pronunciation of the Tetragrammaton, God's actual name, should remain secret knowledge, because it is too powerful for ordinary folk. The big question is the אד pronunciation, *Adonai*. Is it too close to the secret source, inviting the possibility of use, or not? We of course know the answer, because we've been saying *Adonai* in our *brakhot* all our lives. How *Adonai* won out is a story we can't trace any more finely than we've done here. The rest of the story, the final victory, was never recorded or preserved.

## Conclusion

When we begin our *brakhot* בָּרוּךְ אַתָּה יהוה, we are asserting our membership in the rabbinic revolution. We are taking part of

the power that once belonged to the High Priest and assigning
it to every Jew. It is the extension of an old biblical idea, the
expression that we are a "Kingdom of Priests and a Holy
People." It is part of the same populous revolt that made every
dining room and kitchen table (and perhaps even every T.V.
tray) an altar and every synagogue a place where the *Shekhinah*,
God's neighborly presence, resides. It is a complete decentral-
ization of the Holy. When you say *Adonai*, you are saying, "I
don't need an intermediary between God and me—I dial
direct." *Adonai* is a revolutionary call, a statement of pride and
privilege.

There is still more I do not know, secrets about the universe
that I am yet to learn. If I learn them, I will know more about
how to live closely with God. Even so, in each of the 100 little
actions I do every day, actions that trigger 100 little *brakhah*
statements, I am coming close to doing what the *Kohein
ha-Gadol* could do only once a year. I am continuing the
revolution of the ever-evolving Torah.

Pass the garlic, please.

# 7

# Desired Ambivalence

**The function of the *Malkhut*: The God descripter, *Elohim*, defines God as a Judge. Its use in the *Malkhut* section connects The Creater-of-the-Cosmos to the creation of universal ethics. Each of the names we call God (*Shem* and *Malkhut*) not only defines an aspect of God (or an aspect of our relationship with God) but also a set of obligations. The use of *Adonai* involves us in *Ol ha-Mitzvot* (The "Yoke" of the *Mitzvot*), while the use of *Elohim* involves us in *Ol Malkhut Shamayim* (The "Yoke" of God's Cosmic Rulership).**

## A Talmudic Trailer: *Sanhedrin* 59a

Rabbi
Yohanan:  A non-Jew who studies Torah deserves to die.

Rabbi
Meir:          A non-Jew who studies Torah is as holy as the
               High Priest.[1]

Curious? Angry? Want to understand? Read this section!


## A Review

In our exploration of the God name, *Adonai*, we learned a lot
about the Hebrew word for God, *Elohim*.

a. *Elohim* is a job description. It is the role "god"; even pagan
   gods are called *Elohim*.

b. The word *Elohim* also means judge. The Torah even uses it
   (on a couple of occasions) to refer to human judges.

c. The use of *Elohim* evokes one set of relationships with God.

   1. *Elohim* is the God of creation.

   2. *Elohim* is the universal God, the God available to all
      people.

   3. *Elohim* is the God who can be discovered in logic and in
      nature.

d. Each of these aspects of being *Elohim* has a parallel set of
   *Adonai* attributes, reflecting the duality of Jewish religious
   experience.

---

[1]Here, the use of High Priest is serious, designed to indicate the
holiest person in Israel. For the moment, forget everything we
learned in the last section about the rabbis trying to undercut the
priesthood. The rabbis were never sarcastic. In this context, they are
taking the High Priest seriously. They are suggesting that a non-Jew
who studies Torah is as holy as the holiest Israelite.

In this section, we are going to look at the obligations that come with using each of these God names. We have already suggested that each of these names evokes not only an experience of God, but a specific relationship with God. Each of those relationships comes with responsibilities.

In order to understand this process, we need to look back at *midrash* and recomprehend a series of biblical events we've known about since childhood.

## A Midrashic Sound Bite:

Here is a small section of *Genesis Rabbah* 30:9, an extended midrashic sermon on God as Law Giver (which we will study in full later in this chapter). It addresses the distinction between the moral laws that all people (regardless of race, creed, nationality, gender, sexual preference, etc.) should follow, and those that are unique for the Jewish people. In the end, we'll learn that the *Elohim* relationship binds all people to follow seven basic commandments, while the *Adonai* relationship commits Jews to 613.

> God gave Adam six commandments.
> God added one for Noah.
> Abraham had eight.
> And Jacob had nine.
> But to Israel, God gave them all.

The basic concept here is simple: first God gave some basic law codes to humanity; and then, later, God gave an extended, specific, detailed human operating manual to the Jewish people. This notion evolves into a concept that the rabbinic tradition labels *sheva mitzvot b'nai Noah*, the seven *mitzvot* of the Children of Noah.

Here is the way this progression is developed. God taught Adam six *mitzvot*. According to the Talmud, *Sanhedrin* 56a, these are:

1. Establishing courts

2. Refraining from blasphemy

3. Refraining from idolatry

4. Refraining from sexual misconduct (incest, adultery, pederasty, and bestiality)

5. Refraining from murder

6. Refraining from stealing.

Adam and Eve were not permitted to eat meat. Noah and his children were. So, to Noah God gave an additional commandment, "You may not cut a limb from a living animal." Next, Abraham then received his own *mitzvah*: circumcision. Jacob received his own *mitzvah*, too; his was a prohibition to eat from the hindquarters of an animal (the same part of his leg that was stressed in his fight at the Jabbok river). Finally, Israel arrives at Mount Sinai, makes a covenant, and receives the Torah with all 613 of the *mitzvot*.

Ethically, this suggests that there are seven quintessential *mitzvot*, the seven given to Noah. These are universal—rules by which all people must live—rules by which all people are to be judged. In other words, in this process of legal evolution, the *midrash* is placing both an obligation (for essential goodness) and a possibility of ethical accomplishment (living up to God's expectations) on all humanity.

In the next stage of ethical evolution, a very basic proto-Judaism emerges with Abraham's covenant and circumcision, expands very slightly with Jacob's Godwrestling,[2] and comes to fruition at Mount Sinai.

This entire progression of ethical evolution is essentially midrashic. Even though it echoes a thematic sense evident in the biblical text, its ties to the actual biblical text are tenuous.

---

[2]Godwrestler is an English rendition of the Hebrew, *Yisrael*, created by my teacher and friend Arthur Waskow, as an explanation of Jacob's transformation that night at the Jabbok river.

More because it is an interesting passage than because it is a necessary passage, we are next going to take a look at *Genesis Rabbah* 15:6, the passage that establishes Noah's seven *mitzvot*. It allows us to witness much of the process in action.

### *Midrash* at Work: A Training Tangent

Before we read this piece of *midrash*, here is one clue. The form of reasoning used here is a principle of interpretation called *gezeirah shavah*. It involves finding the same word in two passages and then interconnecting their meaning. It is the biblical equivalent of the following mathematical principle:

$$If\ x + y = z$$
$$And\ x + n = z$$
$$Then,\ n = y$$

As you read, forget the logic about which came first. Forget that Adam and Eve couldn't possibly decode these *mitzvot*, that they couldn't know about Hosea, or even Noah. Just enjoy it as a kind of intellectual play—that's exactly what the rabbis did. They were busy establishing "moral truths," not history.

## The *Midrash*: *Genesis Rabbah* 15:6

וַיְצַו יהוה אֱלֹהִים עַל־הָאָדָם לֵאמֹר מִכֹּל עֵץ־הַגָּן אָכֹל תֹּאכֵל

And *Adonai*, The God
Commanded Adam (The Man) saying:
of every tree of the Garden you may freely eat.

Genesis 2:16

Rabbi Levi said: [This verse shows us that] God taught Adam six commandments. [Each word is a clue.]

1. From the word וַיְצַו *Va-yitzav* [Commanded] we learn that God forbad idolatry. This can be learned by looking at Hosea 5:11: "Ephraim is oppressed and crushed by My

judgment because they walked after צָו *Tzav* [meaning idols]."

2. From the word יהוה *Adonai* we can learn that one cannot blaspheme God. This can be learned by looking at Leviticus 24:16: "One who blasphemes the name of יהוה *Adonai* Shall be put to death."

3. From the word אֱלֹהִים *Elohim* we can learn the need to establish courts. This can be learned by looking at Exodus 22:27: "You shall not offend אֱלֹהִים *Elohim* [meaning judges]."

4. From the word הָאָדָם *ha-Adam* [the man] we can learn that murder is forbidden. This can be learned by looking at Genesis 9:6: "Who sheds blood of הָאָדָם [a man], by a man shall his blood be shed."

5. From the words "of every tree of the garden you may freely eat," we learn that the theft is forbidden, because Adam was to eat freely, not steal.

6. And from the entire phrase, "And *Adonai*, the God, commanded Adam," we learn that incest and adultery was forbidden. . . . We know this from the first thing God commanded after Eve was created (Genesis 2:23): "A man leaves his father and mother and cleaves to his wife."

The reasoning here is simple. In the middle of the story of Adam and Eve, the Torah uses the word "commanded" for the first time. The rabbis don't take commandments lightly; after all, *mitzvot* are important to them. They conclude that if the word "commanded" is used, we are indeed talking *mitzvot*, commandments—not suggestions or guidelines. Therefore, because God commanded Adam, some of the 613 *mitzvot* must be intended for all of Adam's decedents (humanity at large).

As they think about it, they come up with six candidate *mitzvot* that are then midrashically reinserted (as a foreshadowing of the Sinaitic revelation) earlier in the biblical text using *gezeirah shavah*.

Four of these *mitzvot* are reasonably obviously choices. They are *mitzvot* of social justice, and reasonably form the core of a communal law code: courts, murder, robbery, and sex crimes. Given the presence of these ethical factors, an essentially just society is likely to emerge. Two of these *mitzvot*, however, at first seem like strange selections because blasphemy against God and idolatry have to do with faith, not interpersonal ethics. In that sense they violate our expectations. It is this disjunction, this insertion of a level of spiritual awareness, that is truly interesting.

Contrary to our initial assumption that to be a "good person," non-Jews simply have to "be fair" and not hurt anyone, these two *mitzvot* suggest that to be ethical, a person must have a basic belief in God (or at least not hold errors about God's reality). These *mitzvot* seem to reflect a notion, frequently popularized by Dennis Prager in his lectures and on his radio show: "If I don't believe in God, then I am setting myself up as God."[3] In other words, a society that denies the existence of a Creator, and believes that it can create the gods, won't be ethical (it is highly unlikely to be ethical—I would hate to offend a sincere secular humanist). This is what the rabbis call *Ol Malkhut Shamayim*, the acknowledgment of the Rulership of The Cosmic-Creator.

This God as universal *Melekh* is exactly the relationship described by Yehuda ha-Levi as *Elohim*, the God of Aristotle. It is this universally mandated understanding of God as Cosmic Creator and Ruler that motivates the *Malkhut* section of the *brakhah* formula:

אֱלֹהֵינוּ מֶלֶךְ הָעוֹלָם

*Eloheinu Melekh ha-Olam*
**Our God, The Ruler-of-the-Cosmos**

*Elohim* is the God of every person, and it is right and proper for every person to have an awareness of and a connection to *Elohim*.

---

[3]This is a comment I have frequently heard Dennis make in both his public teaching and from his radio platform.

## A Rabbinic Ambivalence: *Sanhedrin* 59a

Take a look at this small section of Talmud, *Sanhedrin* 59a. Its argument reveals something interesting. As you read, notice the centrality of Noah's seven *mitzvot* to this whole discussion.

Rabbi
Yohanan:    A non-Jew who studies the Torah deserves to die, for it is taught [in Deuteronomy 33:4]:

Torah:       "Moses commanded us Torah as an inheritance."

Rabbi
Yohanan:    [Torah] is our inheritance, not theirs. [By studying it, is like stealing it from us. For that they deserve death.]

A Rabbi:    Then why wasn't this prohibition also included in the seven *mitzvot* given to Noah?

Rabbi
Meir:        We've been taught, "A non-Jew who studies the Torah is as holy as the *Kohein ha-Gadol*. It comes from [Leviticus 8:5]:

Torah:       "You shall therefore keep My statutes and My judgments, by following these, a **person** shall **live**.

Rabbi
Meir:        [The Torah] doesn't say "a priest," it doesn't say "a Levite," it doesn't even say "an Israelite"—it just says "a **person**"—therefore "any person" who studies Torah is equal to the *Kohein ha-Gadol*.

Rabbi:       I think that non-Jews should be limited to portions that involve the seven *mitzvot* of Noah [the laws they are responsible to enact].

Ambivalence is fun. Ambivalence is honest. Ambivalence is human. Ambivalence is Jewish. And, especially, ambivalence is rabbinic. What we have in this passage are diverse sentiments about non-Jews.

Rabbi Yohanan reflects an animosity. We can read into it years of anti-Semitism, lots of fear, hatred, resentment, etc.—real experience in dealing with Egyptians, Canaanites, Assyrians, Babylonians, Persians, Greeks, Romans, etc. Jews have good reason to resent non-Jews and to keep our one special treasure proprietorially ours.

Rabbi Meir, however, reflects an understanding that all people are God's children, and in a sense, while we are the "chosen" recipients of Torah, it is something that should come to serve all people.

The irony in this *Gemara* fragment is that both sides are forced to root their approach to non-Jews in Noah's sons' seven *mitzvot*. For Rabbi Yohanan, they are a limit. He dares non-Jews to cross the line and perform or examine more than their limits. For Rabbi Meir, these seven *mitzvot* are a foundation, the starting point on which a universal, messianic, ethical future will be built.

## A Profound Rabbinic Ambivalence:
*Exodus Rabbah* 30:9

Near the top of this section we saw a small piece of *midrash* that described the evolution of the revealed *mitzvot*. Now we're going to work our way through the entire passage that contains it. Not only will it give us a deeper sense of the relationship between "universal" and "Jewish" *mitzvot*, but it will also expose us to a much deeper sense of this Jewish ambivalence toward non-Jews.

**Meet the Proem: An Introductory Training Tangent**

*Midrash* comes in two basic flavors: homiletical (sermonic) and exegetical (explanatory). Homiletical *midrash* actually started out as public sermons. Exegetical *midrash* followed a text through line by line, commenting on individual phrases.

We are about to read a piece of homiletic *midrash*, a sermon. Homiletic *midrash* has a fairly rigid structural pattern. The opening part of each of the chapters of *Midrash Rabbah* is made up of a series of sermons. In Aramaic, each of these sermons is called a *pitikta* (an opening). In English, they go by the technical term, *proem*. The goal of a *pitikta* is to explain the meaning of one verse by connecting it to a second verse. Usually, the verse being explained comes from the Torah. Usually, the "proem verse," the one to which it is compared, comes from *Nakh* [an acronym for the *Nivi'im* (Prophets) and *Ketuvim* (Writings)].

A *pitikta* will open with the biblical verse and then state the proem verse. Next, a series of intermediary explorations will expose facets of the connection between the two. Then it will conclude by fully drawing the two verses together.

**The Biblical Text: Exodus 21:1**

In Chapter 20 of Exodus, God gives the Torah to Israel. Starting in Chapter 21, God teaches Moses a basic code of Jewish law, sometimes called "The Book of the Covenant." In the two chapters that follow, we are taught a basic code of Civil Law, the ways people should live together. Included are such topics as property rights, damages, personal injury, laws of slavery, murder, self-defense, manslaughter, etc. This verse is its opening sentence in this process.

> "Now these are the *mishpatim* [judgments]
> which you shall put before them."

In looking at this verse, there are many questions to ask. This particular sermon, however, will ultimately focus on the relationship between these codes of ethics and the Jewish people.

The question being asked is, "If the rules that follow are really the 'universal truth' about what is just and how people should live in communities, why did God give them only to the Jewish people? Shouldn't God have revealed these basic ethical considerations to everyone, and given us the esoteric stuff (like access to mystical power via God's forty-two-letter name)?"

## The Proem Verse: Psalm 147:19-20

(a) "He tells his דְּבָרָו *Davar* [word] to Jacob
(b) חֻקָּיו *Huk-kav* [His statutes]
מִשְׁפָּטָיו *U'Mishpatav* [And His judgments] to Israel.
(a) He didn't do this for any of the other Nations
(b) His מִשְׁפָּטִים *Mishpatim* [judgments] they have not known. Hallelujah."

The Psalms are a collection of hymns of praise to God, many of them pieces of the actual Temple liturgy sung by Levites as part of the daily service. In this case, we are looking at the last two verses of the next-to-last psalm.

Psalms are instances of biblical poetry. Rather than focusing on rhymes, biblical poems form couplets in another way. They say the same thing twice in two different ways.[4] A famous example you know well is:

(a) "They shall beat their **swords** into **plowshares**,
(b) their **spears** into pruning **hooks**.
(a) **Nation** shall not **lift up sword** against nation,
(b) neither shall they **learn war** any more."

In this case (and the same is true for our proem-verse), the (b) part of the verse restates the (a) statement. The artistry in biblical poetry comes in the ability to create such couplets.

---

[4]At the moment there is a lot of scholarly debate over the exact nature of these couplets. Robert Alter, in his book, *The Art of Biblical Poetry* (New York: Basic Books, 1985), suggests that the second line is a kind of intensifier, a grander or more significant follow-up. But for our brief purposes, our simple understanding will do.

Artistry in midrashic interpretation comes in proving that both halves of the couplet actually teach different lessons.

In the proem verse we encounter three technical terms: דָּבָר davar (word), חֹק hok (statute), and מִשְׁפָּט mishpat (judgment). To our ear, they are all synonyms for the laws revealed in the Torah. That's fine in English literature, but to the rabbinic ear, they create a problem. They assume (for some reasons we won't go into here) that every phrase in the Bible must convey a new, unique, important meaning. Nothing is ever repeated for style or for effect—everything has meaning. Therefore, one of their early tasks in this midrash is to explain the difference between these terms.

Later, this proem verse will trigger our essential question: "Why did God hold back the majority of the ethical laws from the remainder of humankind?"

## The Midrash: Exodus Rabbah 30:9

Another explanation of:
**"Now these are the judgments"**

**a.**

It is written in Psalm 147:19–20:
**"He tells his דָּבָר [word] to Jacob."**
Davar [word] means the Ten Commandments (עֲשֶׂרֶת הַדִּבְּרוֹת, Asseret ha-Dibrot).
"חֻקָּיו [His statutes] וּמִשְׁפָּטָיו [And His judgments] to Israel."
This means His judgments.[5]

---

[5]Commenting on Leviticus 11:3–4, Rashi clarifies the difference between mishphatim and hukkim.

Mishpatim: These refer to the mitzvot of justice stated in the Torah of justice. If they had not been stated there, they should have been.

Hukkim: These are the mitzvot that are royal decrees about which the evil inclination raises objections why we should observe them at all, and regarding which the Gentiles taunt us, such as the eating of pork and the wearing of Sha'atnez (mixing wool and flax).

**"Now these are the judgments that you [Moses] shall put before them The [Families of Israel]"** is our Torah text. Only the first part of the verse is quoted, because it is expected that you will know the rest of it by heart. In those days everyone did.

**"He tells his word To Jacob . . ."** is our proem-verse. The initial connection here is obvious—in the Torah text, God instructs Moses to begin teaching the day-to-day laws (*mishpatim*) for the first time. In the proem verse we learn that these day-to-day laws are the exclusive inheritance of the Jewish people. The entire *midrash* will explore the reasons that these *mishpatim* are exclusive rather than universal.

Even before we start into this *midrash*, one part of the connection between these two verses is obvious—the word *misphatim* connects the texts. It is part of each, and for the rabbis, that overlap draws the two verses together. We begin with a statement about God that seems to have no connection to our topic.

**b.**

God does things differently from people.
One person will order another,
to do something that he, himself, will not do.
But God only tells Israel to do and observe those things
which God (Himself)[6] also does.

**c.**

A story about Rabban Gamliel, Rabbi Joshua, Rabbi Eliezer ben
     Azaria, and Rabbi Akiva.
They went to Rome and taught there:

---

[6]The translation of this piece of *Midrash* uses masculine pronouns. My skill is not facile enough to render it in a nonsexist form while preserving a sense of ready access. Please accept the fact (as I noted earlier in this manuscript) that while masculine God language, and a generalized use of "He" for people was the rabbinic norm, it need not be our present understanding.

"God does things differently than people do.
People enjoy ordering others around while doing nothing
    themselves—
God doesn't work that way."


An apostate Jew was listening to them,
and heckled them as they were leaving with this question:
"Didn't you just say that God says a thing and fulfills it.
[If that is the case] why doesn't God observe the *Shabbat*
    prohibitions?
[After all, doesn't God cause the wind to carry things
from one place to another on *Shabbat*.][7]


"Fool!" they answered him, "Isn't a person permitted to carry
    things within his own courtyard on *Shabbat*?
He answered, "Yes."
Then they told him, "Both the upper and lower regions are the
    courtyard of God. We learn this from [Isaiah 6:3]:
'The whole earth is full of His Glory. . . .' "

The portion of the *midrash* we've labeled "b" states a general
principle. The "c" portion is a story, explaining the principle
and connecting it to our topic.

The basic principle is that the Torah's laws are cosmic, not
just human. God is directly involved in the life of these laws.
God is not just a lawgiver, but also a legal actualizer. Essentially, God's true nature is more *Adonai*, looking for a partnership with Israel, than *Elohim*, The Universal-Creator-of-all.

The story is basically a morality play. It stars the four rabbinic
horsemen in white *kippot*. Its villain is a *min* (probably by
context), a Jew who has converted to Christianity. The story
goes like this: The good guys go to Rome, the capitol of evil,
and give the good message, "God lives Torah." An apostate, a
Jew who has been seduced to serve evil, tries to embarrass
them and mock their truth. The apostate (probably Black Beryl)

---

[7]One of the forty-nine forbidden acts of labor on *Shabbat* is carrying
things from one domain to another.

thinks he can beat them on their own turf, Jewish law, but in this showdown at the O.K. Coliseum, they shut him down cold.

The truth of truths being taught here is that once you are inside the rabbinic process, the true truth always emerges. That is why God gave the Torah exclusively to Israel. Unless you invest fully in the process, it is easy to misuse the law.

In part "d," we go for the next explanation of the connection between these two verses. This time, the explanation will use a favorite rabbinic midrashic format, the parable. Even though the story doesn't end Q.E.D., it does directly explain, "His *mishpatim* they have not known."

**d.**

Another explanation of:
**"He tells his word to Jacob."**
Rabbi Abbahu taught in the name of Rabbi Yose b. Hanina:

This can be compared to a king who had an orchard.
In it he planted all kinds of trees.
He was the only one who entered this garden—
he, himself, was its keeper.
When his children came of age, he said to them:
"My children,
up to now I guarded this garden.
I didn't allow anyone else to enter it.
Now, I want you to keep this garden as I have."

The parable here is easy:

King = God.<br>
King's children = Children of Israel<br>
Garden of Trees = Torah

The Torah is of course considered to be "the Tree of Life." But a garden of trees is also Torah.

In Hebrew, the word for an orchard (a garden of trees) is פַּרְדֵּס
*Pardais*. The English word *Paradise* comes from an Arabic form
of the same word stem. In rabbinic symbolism, פַּרְדֵּ״ם stands for
the four layers of meaning that can be extracted from a Torah
text. פ = *Peshat*, the plain meaning. ר = *Remez*, the clues about
future history. ד = *Drash* (as in *Midrash*), the interpretive
meaning. ם = *Sod*, the hidden or mystical meaning.

Keeping = Keeping

Keeping is a basic Jewish behavior. God put people in the
garden (of Eden) "to work it and to keep it" (Genesis 2:15).
Cain is told to be "his brother's keeper" (Genesis 4:9). Abraham
is described as one who will teach his family "to keep *Adonai's*
way—to do what is just and right" (Genesis 18:19).

Next, the *midrash* explains the parable, by applying it to God
and Israel.

**e.**

This is what God [the King] said to Israel [His Children]:
"Prior to My creation of the cosmos, I prepared the Torah,
that is the meaning of Proverbs 8:30:
**'I was with Him as an** אָמוֹן *amon* **[nursling]'**—this means 'a
   tutor.'
'It is explained by comparison with Numbers 11:12:
**'As an** אֹמֵן *oman* **[nursing father] carries a sucking child.'**
I did not give the Torah to heathens,
rather I gave to Israel as soon as they said (Exodus 24:7):
**'All *Adonai* has Spoken, we will do and we will obey.'"**

This is the meaning of:
**"He tells his word to Jacob**
His statutes And His judgments to Israel."

**"He didn't do this for any of the other Nations.**
His judgments they have not known.
Hallelujah."

Only Jacob,[8] whom God chose from all the heathen peoples,
received the whole Torah [all 613 commandments].
God gave Adam six commandments.
God added one for Noah.
Abraham had eight.
And Jacob had nine.
But to Israel, God gave them all.

The core of this portion, the "proof" that the Torah was created
before the rest of creation, is very complex, and it is involved in
a number of Hebrew word plays. The material here is a brief
reworking of the opening *midrash* of *Genesis Rabbah*. To understand it, we need to look at the book of Proverbs. There it says:

*Adonai* created me as the beginning of His paths
the first of His works of old.
For eternity I was established first,
I preceded the *creation* of the earth. . . .

I was with him as an אָמֹן *oman*
and I was his daily delight.

What we learn from examining the whole passage from Proverbs is that the narrator, the "I," was clearly the first thing
created. In the context in Proverbs (more than I've quoted
above), it becomes evident that the narrator, the "I," is Wisdom
speaking. In the parallel passage in *Genesis Rabbah* (the one
being glossed here) Wisdom is turned into Torah with one
sentence: "There is no wisdom except for Torah." Therefore,
the Torah precedes creation.

The second verse being cited is being quoted for the sake of
word use, not context. It actually comes from a speech where
Moses loses his cool and blows up at God. The context is
mid-way through the forty years in the wilderness, and the
people are again complaining about their diet.

---

[8]God changed Jacob's name to Israel. Here the reference is not to
the man, Jacob, but his offspring, the nation of Israel.

You have put [the whole] burden for this people on me.
Did I conceive all this people?
Did I give birth to them?
Yet, You said to me:
"Carry them in your bosom as an אמן *oman* carries an infant—
to the land that You have promised in an oath to their
    fathers. . . ."

In citing this verse, the rabbis are just "proving" that *oman*
stands for a nurse. In other words, this *midrash* has the Torah
say, "I was the nurse God created [to help raise the Jewish
people]." This then leads us to the remainder of the passage,
which establishes the proprietary relationship between Torah
(all 613 *mitzvot*) and Israel. The important insight here is that
the Jewish people qualify for the gift by saying: "All *Adonai* has
spoken, we will do and we will obey." This is an echo of a
famous *midrash* (*Mekhilta, Yitro* 5) where God offers the Torah
to each of the other nations of the world. Each of these nations
asks for some example of the Torah's content before they
would accept it. To each, God rereveals one of the seven
commandments given to Noah. (These are commandments
they are already supposed to follow.) Based on a *mitzvah* (to
which they are already subject), each nation rejects the Torah
as being too restrictive. Finally, God offers the Torah to Israel,
and without questioning its content at all, Israel says, "We will
do—and we will listen." Because they gave blind obedience,
offering to "do" before "hearing," they are considered the
"choosing people," therefore worthy of being "chosen." The
use of "All *Adonai* has spoken, we will do and we will obey"
captures this same sense of Israel's uniqueness meriting the
Torah as their nurse.

Finally, this is all fully explained in terms of the "chain of the
*mitzvot*" that we examined earlier in this chapter.

Then, we move on to more parables.

**f.**

Rabbi Simon said in the name of Rabbi Hanina:
"It can be compared to a king who sat at a banquet table

set with all kinds of dishes.
When his first servant entered, he gave him a slice of meat.
When the second entered, he gave him an egg.
When the third entered, he gave some vegetables.
He gave a portion to each one separately.
When his son came in, he gave him all that was before him,
saying to him:
'To the others I gave only a single portion, but to you I give all.'

"So also God gave the heathen only some odd commandments,
but when Israel arose, God said to them:
'Behold, the whole Torah is yours.'
This is the meaning of:
**'He didn't do this for any of the other Nations.'** "

Once again, we are using a king metaphor for a parable. The
notion here is that this king is king to all, even giving his
servants food from his plate (a real honor). However, the king
has a special relationship with one servant, his son. So, too,
God is God to all and reveals God's will to all, but God has a
special relationship with Israel, the chosen people. Despite
what others say, we are like the son God never had.

And now for another king parable.

### g.

Rabbi Eleazer said:
"It can be compared to a king who went out to war with his
    troops.
When he slaughtered an animal, he would distribute each piece
    proportionally [according to the number in each division].
His son was watching this distribution and asked:
'What [portion] will you give to me?'
The king answered:
'[I will give you] from that which I have prepared myself.'
So God gave to the heathens, commandments as it were, in
    their raw state,
for them to toil over [and actualize],
not making any distinction between uncleanness and purity;

but as Israel came,
God explained each precept separately to them—
the punishment [for not fulfilling it] and its reward.
This is the meaning of Song of Songs 1:2,
**'Let him kiss me with the kisses of his mouth.'**


"This is the meaning of:
**'His statutes and His judgments [God Taught] to Israel.'"**

Here, in this final king-and-son parable, we reach a culmination. Here, the image and the issue are completed.

In section "**d**," God is like a king who guards an orchard, the Torah. The responsibility for the future of this orchard is then passed to the next in line, Israel. The metaphor here is that Torah is a living thing. As keepers we are responsible for both preserving the living aspects of Jewish law and providing for new growth. An orchard, like the law, is an evolving, growing entity based on solid, old roots, deep roots.

In section "**d**," however, non-Jews have no contact with Torah. In fact, they are not even considered. The garden is guarded, in essence, to keep them out. This *midrash* echoes Rabbi Yohanan's condemnation of non-Jews learning Torah.

In section "**e**," God is like a king who feeds his servants (all humanity) from his own nourishment, food. To each, God gives a token of love—to Israel, the Prince (of nations), God gives a well-balanced, complete meal, not just a symbolic morsel. In the first metaphor, the nations have no part in the Torah, the seven Noachian laws are not even considered. Here, they are considered tokens of affection, not a viable system.

In section "**f**," God is like a king leading an army. As a responsible king, each troop is given what it needs, only his son is given a hand-prepared portion. Here, if we extend the metaphor fully, the ethical laws of the Torah—the real keys to *mishpat* (a just society)—are available to all people. (Think of "the God of Aristotle," Who reveals Truth through logic and nature.) What distinguishes the Torah is "love." The Torah is personally prepared as an act of love. As the quote from Song of Songs, "Let him kiss me with the kisses of his mouth," establishes, Torah is like a kiss from God's mouth. The differ-ence is the logic behind the laws (the punishments and rewards) and the process of personal interest.

In this last section, we get a new vision. Here, God doesn't withhold anything from the rest of humankind (God doesn't withhold a well-balanced ethical diet or keep them out of the garden). Instead, all is available, but Israel gets a loving, personal introduction to each and every facet. Here, all peoples are "good," and the nation of Israel is "very good."

## A Review:

1. The *Malkhut* section involves (a) using God's name *Elohim* (the job description) and (b) mentioning that God is *Melekh ha-Olam* (The Ruler-of-the-Cosmos).

2. The name *Elohim* implies three things, (a) that God is a Judge (*Midat ha-Din*); (b) that God is the Universal Creator (transcendent); and (c) that God is accessible to all people (what Yehuda ha-Levi calls "the God of Aristotle").

3. The *Malkhut* section is connected to the acceptance of God as The Ruler-of-the-Cosmos *(Ol Malkhut Shamayim)*.

4. God's revelation of Justice came in two basic thrusts, seven *mitzvot* to Noah's children (all of humanity) and 613 *mitzvot* (the whole Torah) to the Jewish people.

What we have found interesting in this exploration is the ambivalence felt in the Jewish tradition toward "the Nations." Essentially the question is, "If we are better (because we are 'chosen')—are 'they' worse?" What we've found is three an-swers: "yes," "no," and "well, maybe." There are many ways to explain this ambivalence, but the usual is to assume that what we have received, now, they will recognize later. This is best expressed in the Isaiah 2:1–4:

And it will come to be in the end of days
that the mountain with *Adonai's* house

will be the top, above all of the mountains
and it will be praised more than any other hill
and all nations shall flow to it
and many people shall go and say:

"Come, let us go up to *Adonai*'s mountain
to Jacob's God's House.

And He will teach us of His ways
And we will walk in His paths

For out of Zion will Torah be broadcast—
And the *Adonai*'s word from Jerusalem."[9]

This passage is clearly messianic. It deals with the future, not
the present. Yet, while Torah may be exclusively for the Jewish
people at the moment (our own little Paradise), its final end is
clearly universal. Therefore, at some point, the seven *mitzvot*
must grow into a well-explained, well-balanced meal. That is
the root of the ambivalence found in the *midrashim* and
talmudic selections we have seen. On the one hand, we have
had a history of poor experiences dealing with the other
nations (remember, all of this is written more than a thousand
years before the enlightenment), and it is hard to see them
respecting or adopting this material (they have enough trouble
with the seven *mitzvot*). On the other hand, ultimately, we have
been told that they will come to learn and cherish this material.
In his book, *Worship and Ethics*, Max Kadushin[10] describes it
this way:

As it combines with other concepts, *Malkhut Shamayim*, we
learned, signifies that God's dominion is everywhere, that God
will ultimately be recognized as King by the whole world, that it

_____

[9]Before we analyze this passage, notice the poetic parallelism.
[10]Max Kadushin, *Worship and Ethics, A Study in Rabbinic Judaism*
(Evanston, IL: Northwestern University Press, 1964), p. 49.

negates basically the dominion of the Nations of the World over Israel, that it is acknowledged after experiencing God's love or mercy, that it immediately implies the observance of the *mitzvot*.

## Closure

In *Mishnah Brakhot* 2:2 we find this passage:

> One should first acknowledge that God is The Ruler-of-the-Cosmos (*Ol Malkhut Shamayim*)
> and then acknowledge the obligation for the commandments (*Ol ha-mitzvot*).

The classic explanation here is that first you accept God as the overall authority, the One who has the right to command, and then you accept the actual commandments. This is a direct echo of *na'aseh venishma*. (If you ask it of us, we'll say yes first, and then hear the particulars later.)

I believe that there is a second consideration here, one conveyed by the spiritual aspect of the seven *mitzvot* given to all people.

As a Jew, I have two relationships with God—one as a member of humanity and one as a Jew. I need to see myself as special and unique; and I need to see myself as ordinary. It is this balance that keeps "chosenness" from becoming apartheid. The use of *Elohim* reminds me that, despite my privilege, I am still part of a larger whole. The double-name formula in the *brakhah* formula, *Shem* and *Malkhut*, make each religious act an affirmation of my unique family history and the obligations it carries—*Ol ha-Torah*, and they make each moment of blessing an affirmation of humble status as one member of humankind, struggling, like everyone else, with the basics—*Ol Malkhut Shamayim*. After all, all of us are God's children; princes and princesses are people, too.

# 8

# Eating the Ethical

**Saying a *brakhah* impacts upon us two ways: spiritually and ethically. It is like shining a spot light and focusing our gratitude. It is like looking in a mirror and adjusting the way we are living up to God's image.**

## Two Experiences in One

My friend and teacher, Rabbi Larry Mahrer, is fond of teaching an important rabbinic lesson by quoting an old Baptist preacher:

A religion which ain't no good on Monday,
ain't no good on Sunday.

Its meaning is deep. On the surface it says, "If going to church on Sunday doesn't make you act ethically on Monday, then it is a meaningless action." However, it says much more. It suggests that religion is more than worship and ceremonial

117

actions, more than the times set aside for religious participation, more than any single part. Religion is supposed to be a whole. This simple statement attacks the entire dichotomy by which most of us live secular lives, interrupted by and perhaps even animated by religious respites. We have a great tendency to reduce religion (and especially Jewishness) to a leisure-time activity (in competition with golf and tennis, not our livelihoods). For Rabbi Larry, the issue is always ethics: if religious activities (ceremonies) don't empower religious actions (ethics), then religious involvement is meaningless. For him, real Judaism has everything to do with business and other day-to-day experiences.

Another one of my friends and teachers, Rabbi Yosi Gordon, likes to stress the other side of this connection. He attacks the "secular" dichotomy by saying, "If ethical actions are just good deeds, then they aren't *mitzvot*; to be *mitzvot*, one must encounter God." If he was the Baptist preacher, he would preach:

A religion which ain't no good on Sunday,
ain't no good on Monday.

As far as the rabbis go, both of them are right.

This sense of the continual interweaving of the ethical (interpersonal actions) and the spiritual (encounters with God) is at the core of the Judaism the rabbis evolved. They spun the Torah's fabric into a *mitzvah*-system, shaping it into an organic whole where these distinctions, the dichotomy we find so comforting (because it is so much less demanding), is completely hidden in the tight weave. When it comes to *mitzvot*, symbolic actions are impossible to distinguish from actions that make a real impact. Actions that are designed to be "training" or "preparation" can't be separated from those that represent actual fulfillment.

In many ways, *brakhot* are the magic words that animate the *mitzvah*-system and bring rabbinic Judaism, our Judaism, to life. It is through the saying of *brakhot* that ordinary actions are raised to spiritual encounters. It is through this fabric of *brakhot* that ethical actions become a continuous flow, not sporadic or short-lived involvements.

In this section, we are going to unravel a little of this intertwining to see how it was accomplished. We are going to examine this slight-of-word in a kind of literary slow motion. In doing so, we will learn much about the richness of a *brakhah*'s double impact.

## Two Metaphors

In working with my own students, I define this twofold religious process through two metaphors:

**Saying a *brakhah* is like shining a spotlight.** When we say a *brakhah*, we focus our attention on an experience or an action, and in the process we turn the potentially mundane into an encounter with the holy. It is a *brakhah* that metamorphizes the lighting of a light into the conjuring of a holy time. It is a *brakhah* that makes the consumption of calories an acknowledgment of God's creative powers and God's loving concern for humankind. Through *brakhot*, such possibly mundane acts as tying shoes, eating something bitter, and even shaking a collection of branches in the air all become opportunities to come closer to God.

**Saying a *brakhah* is like looking in a mirror**. Each and every *brakhah*-saying experience is a moment of self-analysis. *Brakhot* are first (and perhaps foremost) a statement of radical appreciation, an acknowledgment of God's actions. But, they also generate an important side-effect. When these are examined through the conceptual lens of our creation in "God's Image," that which we are praising God for being emerges as that which we will strive to become. Each time we acknowledge that God feeds, or God clothes, or God comforts, or God saves, or God lifts up, we are setting patterns for our own ethical actions: feeding, clothing, comforting, saving, and lifting up.

This same twofold process is the one that Max Kadushin traces in careful detail.[1] He begins his description of this process this way:

---

[1]Max Kadushin, *Worship and Ethics, A Study in Rabbinic Judaism* (Evanston, IL: Northwestern University Press, 1964), p. 46.

All of these acts have a certain character in common. Everyone
of them represents an experience wherein there is felt to be a
manifestation of God in one manner or another. Furthermore,
in all of them that manifestation of God is conveyed by a value
concept.

## Our Journey

One of the latest trends in assembling art exhibits is ar-
ranging them such that they demonstrate the evolution of and
the influences on a given artist's work. Often, an art show will
gather together a series of "alternate" expressions of the same
theme or image, allowing the audience to get a sense of the
development. Others will lay side-by-side teacher and student,
friend and friend, the inspired and the inspiration. In this way
the motivation for—and the inner vision of—a given work or a
given body of work often becomes clear.

In this section we are going to show a number of parallel
expressions of Psalm 24:1:

A Psalm of David

הָאָרֶץ *ha-Aretz* [The Earth/Land] **belongs to** *Adonai*—
**Also all that fills it**—
[This includes] **the world**
**and all who live there.**

For God set its foundations on top of the seas
And established it over the floods.

In this exhibition you will see how this verse simultaneously
is the justification for making all acts of *tzedakah* an obligation,
rather than a voluntary contribution, and the rationale for a
blessing of appreciation to be the mandatory conclusion to
every act of sustenance.

Much of what you see will be predicated on the ability of
the rabbis to see this verse as a *double entendre*. The word

*ha-Aretz* has two distinct meanings: the earth (meaning "the globe") and the Land (meaning "The Land of Israel"). We will see references to *Adonai*'s ownership of each.

## Monday Monday . . .

We begin by examining a display of six biblical *mitzvot* for Jewish farmers. These are the foundation of all the *mitzvot* of *tzedakah*.

### Stop One: A Quick History of Tithing

In the Torah, Jewish farmers are presented with six laws that limited their access to the crops they grow on their own land.

### 1. *Ma'aser*: The First Tenth

"One-tenth (a tithe) of everything that grows in the Land, grains from the ground and fruit from the tree, belongs to *Adonai*; they are holy to *Adonai*" (Leviticus 27:30).

"To the tribe of Levi I give all the tithes in Israel as their share in return for the services they perform" (Numbers 18:21).

### 2. *Ma'aser Sheini*: The Second Tenth

"Each year you should set aside one-tenth of the crop [which remains after the *Ma'aser*]. You eat these tithes . . . before *Adonai*, your God, in the place where God will choose to establish His Name, so that you will learn to be in awe of *Adonai*, your God" (Deuteronomy 14:22–23).

### 3. *Ma'aser Oni*: The Tenth for the Poor

"Every third year, the year of the tithe, After you have set aside one-tenth of your crops And given it to the Levites [take what you would normally use for the *Ma'aser Sheini*] and Give it to the stranger, the orphan, and the widow, that they may eat their fill in your settlements.

"Then, proclaim before *Adonai*, your God: "I have set aside the holy portion for the Temple, and I have given it to the Levite, the stranger, the fatherless, and the widow—just as You commanded me; I have not broken or ignored any of your *mitzvot*. Look down from Your Holy Place, from heaven, and bless Your people, Israel, and the Land You have given us . . . ." (Deuteronomy 26:12–14).

### 4. *Pe'ah*: The Corners

"When you reap the harvest of your fields, you shall not completely harvest the field. Rather, you must leave the corners of the field for the poor and the strangers. I am *Adonai*, Your God" (Leviticus 23:22).

### 5. *Shikheha*: The Forgotten

"When you reap the harvest of your field and you forget a sheaf in the field, do not go back and get it. Leave it for the stranger, the orphan, and the widow—in order that *Adonai*, Your God may bless all that you do" (Deuteronomy 24:19).

### 6. *Leket*: Gleanings

"And when you reap the harvest of your fields, you shall not . . . gather the gleanings of your harvest . . . You shall leave them for the poor and the stranger. I am *Adonai* your God" (Leviticus 19:9–10).

In looking at these seven biblical texts (which give us six *mitzvot*), we learn three things:

1. We get a sense of why the *Mishnah* was necessary. None of these rules is found together. They are spread over three books, yet they clearly intersect. It takes two diverse citations from different locations to learn the rules of *Ma'aser*, a

third citation, from a third location, to learn its connection to *Ma'aser Sheini*, and a fourth citation, from yet another location, to see how all of these intersect with *Ma'aser Oni*. A biblical farmer had no easy way to look up farming rules. This is one reason a subject-oriented code was needed.

2. We learn that a large number of rules apply to biblical farming. A farmer may not keep all of what is grown on his or her farm. A significant portion (on average, more than twenty percent) must be given to Levites, strangers, widows, and orphans.

3. These *mitzvot* have no clear rationale. Unlike other *mitzvot* about strangers, these don't say, as does Exodus 23:9, "For you know the feelings of a stranger, for you yourselves were strangers in the land of Egypt." Instead, these are *mitzvot* just because "God says so." They are justified with the simple statement, "I am *Adonai*, Your God," a biblical rendition of "Because I say so."

In the Talmud, *Yoma* 67b, we find the following:

*Mishpatim*: These are *mitzvot*, which if they were not included in the Torah, should have been. These include: [the laws of] idolatry, sexual impropriety, bloodshed, robbery, and blasphemy.

*Hukkim*: These are the *mitzvot* about which the evil inclination raises objections [why we should at all observe them], such as the wearing of *sha'atnez* (not mixing wool and linen), *halitzah* (a levirite marriage ceremony), the purification of a leper, and the scapegoat. You might think that these are useless things. Therefore, the Torah teaches [in each of these cases], "I Am *Adonai*," [in essence saying, "I] made it a statute [by My authority], you have no right to criticize it."[2]

---

[2]If you want to have a little bit of fun, compare this passage from the Talmud against the Rashi cited in Chapter 4, n. 4. There, you get real insight into his priorities in reworking this passage.

The laws that regard sharing with others the food we raise—
*Ma'aser Oni*, *Pe'ah*, *Shikheha*, and *Leket*—all fall into the latter
category; they are punctuated by "I am *Adonai*."

Next, you will see how the rabbis begin to build a rationale
for these *mitzvot*, evolving a way of explaining their logic.

### Stop Two: *Adonai* is a Good Land-Lord

Here are four rabbinic texts, two *midrashim*, a *mishnah*, and a
small portion of Talmud. Together, they portray a relationship,
which starts by narrowing the focus of the word *Aretz* from
"Earth," meaning world, to "the Land," meaning Israel. Read
in that context, Psalm 24:1 suggests that God has a special
relationship with *Eretz Yisrael*.

### The *Midrash* on Psalm 24:3 (A Fragment)

The Holy-One-Who-Is-to-Be-Blessed:
Created the days [of the week] and took *Shabbat* as God's
    portion,
Created the moon-cycles and chose the festivals as God's
    portion,
Created the years and chose the sabbatical year as God's
    portion,
Created the nations [of the world] and chose Israel as God's
    portion. . . .
Created the lands [of the earth] and took as God's portion
The Land of Israel as a heave-offering from all the other lands:

This is learned from Psalm 24:1:
**"The Land belongs to *Adonai*—also all that fills it."**

This is a straightforward piece of *midrash*. It expresses a
continued echo of the first story of creation. Some things are
"good," a few things are "very good." God's chosen portions
include: *Shabbat*, the festivals, the sabbatical year, the nation of

Israel, and the Land of Israel. The last of these is justified in
terms of our Psalm verse. No implication is yet drawn, just a
special relationship. The implications will follow.

### *Exodus Rabbah* 41:1 (A Fragment)

Next, we will examine a fragment of a larger sermon, a
portion of a proem. The verse that triggers the *midrash* is
Exodus 31:18: "And God gave to Moses, when God had made
an end of speaking with him on Mount Sinai, the two tablets of
the testimony." The original context here is that while the
people of Israel are preparing the Golden Calf, God, cognizant
of their sin, is still willing to complete the revelation of the Ten
Commandments. The proem verse comes from Daniel 9:7: "To
you, *Adonai*, belongs righteousness, but we are shamed." In
other words, we are given gifts beyond our merit. Even when
we deserve punishment, God still rewards us. The Land of
Israel is presented as one of a number of examples in this
pattern:

Rabbi Nehemiah said:

. . . Ordinarily, when one gives a field over to a tenant,
the tenant must supply both the seeds and the labor,
and still the owner receives fifty percent of the produce.
Yet, The Holy-One-Who-Is-to-Be-Blessed—
God's Name is to be praised, God's mention is to be extolled—
doesn't work that way.

We are taught in Psalm 24:1:
**"The Land belongs to *Adonai*—also all that fills it."**

Both the Land and its seeds belong to God,
He also causes the rains to fall,
the dews to spring forth—
these [work] to make the fruit grow and remain fresh.
God does all kinds of work to grow fruit.
Yet God says to Israel:
"I have only commanded you to give me one-tenth . . . as My
   portion."

Here, *Adonai* is described as Israel's Land Lord, and more. While, unlike the Golden Calf and Ten Commandment example to which this is parallel, the nation Israel is not portrayed as doing "shameful" things—the Land of Israel still remains a generous gift, far beyond our merit. Not only does God own the Land (which should entitle God to a payment of half of what is produced), but God also does the bulk of the work to grow the food raised there. For all these efforts, God requests only ten percent. Tithing is payment for using all that God has generously provided. Tithing is the least we should do (and in no way should we ever consider not "paying" our limited fair share).

### Stop Three: The Complications of Putting Ideals into Practice

#### *Pe'ah* 4:9

Strictly speaking, *Pe'ah* (the food left at the corners of the field) isn't a tithe (it's not a fixed tenth of a field), but rather a volunteered, voluntary gift, another one of the obligations that comes with growing food in the Land of Israel. *Pe'ah* doesn't have a fixed amount. Rather, each person decides on his or her own contribution. Only the presence of some kind of corner for those in need is prescribed.

A person who collected the *Pe'ah* [from his field and] said:
"This I have set aside for a specific poor person"—

Rabbi Eliezer says:
"That person has given ownership of that produce to that
   particular poor person."

The sages say:
"[Wrong!] The [owner] must give it to the first poor person
   whom [s/he] meets first."

*Leket, Shikheha,* and *Pe'ah* that belong to a non-Jew must be
   tithed, unless s/he declares them to be public property.

This piece of *Mishnah* offers many complex and confusing insights. The opening portion reinforces the idea that *Pe'ah* is an open offering to all who are in need. Here, the decision follows the sages. Choosing a specific poor recipient doesn't work, because it is then no longer available to all. The *mitzvah* here is to openly provide for all who are in need, not selectively choose our own poor, quasi-poor, or even, perhaps, our relatives.

The last portion of this *Mishnah* is more confusing. To fully understand it, we need some background. This passages plays against the background of Leviticus 25:23–24.

> The Land must not be sold beyond reclaim,
> For the Land is Mine.
> You are only foreigners dwelling with Me.
> In all the Land that you hold,
> you must provide for the redemption of the land.

Every fiftieth year was a Jubilee Year. During that year, all property in the Land of Israel was supposed to return to its original tribal and familiar ownership. This didn't mean that contracts were suddenly voided, that a purchaser who hadn't realized that a Jubilee was coming would be disenfranchised. Rather, it was supposed to become a condition of the sale. Jews who needed money (and therefore were using their property to gain capital) were supposed to either (1) lease their land for a period (and thereby retain ownership) or (2) sell it with a buy-back agreement that was to be actualized on or before the Jubilee. This is the meaning of "you must provide for the redemption of the Land."

In the talmudic passage that follows, you will find the concept of *kinyan perot*, the acquisition of "the fruit rights" of a field, without taking complete ownership. There, the responsibility to tithe will be in question. Here, in the last part of our *Mishnah*, we see a similar question. It works like this.

1. We will assume that the non-Jew in this case has bought rights to use the field for a given period of time, or for a

given outcome. Otherwise, the Jew who sold it to him/her would have violated a *mitzvah*.

2. Because the field is ultimately owned by a Jew, he has an obligation to tithe the field, and especially to tithe the "free-will offerings," which are to be left for other Jews. This is a *kashrut* issue we will explain below. Therefore, to protect Jews who may purchase food grown on this field, it is necessary to either (a) tithe the entire field or (b) declare the food that has been set aside for the needy to be absolutely public property (and therefore not needing a tithe) rather than a gift this individual is offering to the public (which would require a tithe) before it could be considered acceptable for Jewish consumption.

The meaning here is that while the giving of tithes may or may not apply to a non-Jew, the offering of a portion of food to the poor is an obligation placed upon anyone owning land in the Land of Israel. This is a direct ramification of **"The Land belongs to *Adonai*—also all that fills it."**

**Stop Four: More Complications**

### Gittin 47a

The passage that follows is quite difficult. We are only going to deal with a portion of it. Even then, we won't go fully into all of its matters, because there are some complicated laws of possession at work. What we do want to see here are three things.

1. The notion that ownership of property in the Land of Israel comes with special obligations. Because God has gifted us, we must provide for others, even if we sell the property. Our portion of the gift may be given away, but the gift itself must not.

2. Our verse of the day, Psalm 24:1, serves to underpin and support this entire discussion.

3. Psalm 24:1 is placed into dialogue with Psalm 15:6, a verse that seems to say the exact opposite.

### Mishnah

We've talked about the evolution of rabbinic Judaism. And we suggested that much of this emergence stemmed from the growth of a new urban middle class that wanted to work in new ways, but lived by traditional values. *Mishnah* and *Midrash* emerged out of their attempts to update and adapt the Torah to the issues and demands of their new environment.

The seminal book on the early development of these proto-rabbis was a work on the early *havurot*[3] by Jacob Neusner. In it he suggests that two issues, the need to set up an *eruv*[4] for *Shabbat* cooking, and the need to set up a tithing cooperative, were the driving forces in the founding of these early proto-Pharisaic study and practice circles.

To the Pharisees, tithing was important; they made sure that the food they ate had all been tithed (and that *Adonai* had gotten God's due). Often they retithed foods, just to make sure. This concern about tithing underpins this discussion.

If a Jew sells his/her field [in the Land of Israel] to a non-Jew,
the one who purchased it
must still take and bring from it the first fruits,
for the sake of *Tikkun Olam*.

---

[3]Jacob Neusner, *Fellowship in Judaism: The First Century and Today* (London: Vallentine, Mitchell, 1963).

[4]On *Shabbat*, one is forbidden to carry from an inside area to an outside area, or vice versa. A work-around could be achieved, if the outside area was fenced and connected directly and completely to the inside area. This is called an *eruv*. In those days, a courtyard of what was essentially an apartment complex contained the ovens. In order to get hot food inside for *Shabbat*, families living in the courtyard had to cooperate on the construction and maintenance of an *eruv*. This cooperation was often the root of *havurah*.

At first this *Mishnah* seems straightforward. It directly teaches the lesson we would like to learn. Even if a non-Jew buys a field, the obligation to tithe, to give responsibly to the Temple and to those in need, remains in full force. The giving of these gifts leads toward the redemption of the world, *Tikkun Olam*. Unfortunately, as we will see in the *Gemara* that follows, it's not that easy.

## Gemara

### a.

Rabbah:    Even though a non-Jew can purchase property in the Land of Israel, [his or her ownership is not to be complete—even though he or she is not Jewish and therefore subject to Jewish law, the conditions of sale to him/her] must not release the property from the [*mitzvah* of] tithing, since it says in Leviticus 25:23–24:

Torah:    "The Land must not be sold beyond reclaim,
For the Land is Mine.
You are only Foreigners Dwelling with Me.
In all the Land that You hold,
you must provide for the Redemption of the Land."

Rabbah:    "The Land is Mine" essentially says: Its holiness [meaning its tithes,] are Mine; [sales to a non-Jew must not mitigate the obligation to tithe].

        However, a property sale to a non-Jew may give him/her the right to dig pits, ditches, caves, etc. We learn this from the Psalm 15:16:

Bible:    "The heavens are *Adonai*'s heavens.
The earth is given to Adam's children."

Rabbah's interpretation of Leviticus 25:23-24 colors his understanding of everything else. He claims that "For the Land is Mine" means that no matter what else you do with the land, God expects God's ten percent. In other words, the central message of that text, and therefore the meaning of the *Mishnah*, is that no matter who has temporary ownership of the Land, that person (Jew or non-Jew) must follow tithing and related rules—after all, God is the Land Lord, and has set the conditions of occupancy.

Based on this first interpretation, the other uses of the land are irrelevant to Rabbah. It doesn't matter to him what the tenant builds or digs; therefore he cites Psalm 15:16, using it to prove that once one pays the rent, one can do what one pleases. After giving God from "Also, all that fills it," one can say, "The earth is given to Adam's children." The fact that it says "Adam's children" makes it universal, not Jewish. Therefore, a non-Jew can dig and tunnel, etc., in the Land of Israel.

### b.

Rabbi Eliezer takes the opposite position. He sees the tithing rights as part of a Jewish contract with God, a condition of ultimate ownership, not a transferable obligation to a temporary or partial owner.

Rabbi
Eliezer:    [I disagree.] A non-Jew can [be allowed to] own property in the Land of Israel [without retaining the] obligation to tithe. This can be learned from Deuteronomy 14:22–23:

Torah:      "Each year you should set aside one-tenth of the crop. You should eat these tithes before *Adonai*, your God, in the place where God will choose to establish His Name,
            מַעְשַׂר דְּגָנֶךְ
            *Ma'aseh D'ganekha*
            the tithe of your corn,

<table>
<tr><td>Rabbi<br>Eliezer:</td><td>The Torah teaches: "The tithe of your corn," which implies [your corn and] not the corn of non-Jews.<br><br>However, a non-Jew [should not be sold property in the Land of Israel under conditions that allow him or her] to dig pits, ditches, or caves. We learn this from Psalm 24:1:</td></tr>
<tr><td>Bible:</td><td>"The Earth belongs to *Adonai*. . . ."</td></tr>
</table>

the tithe of your wine, the tithe of your oil, the tithe of your firstborn animals, the tithe of your flocks—so that you will learn to be in Awe of *Adonai*, your God."

Rabbi Eliezer reverses both of Rabbah's positions. He says, "Tithes are not the responsibility of a non-Jew, and a non-Jew cannot change or modify God's ground." Interestingly, our verse, which contains the metaphor that has been the background of these discussions, is now played as a card in Rabbi Eliezer's argument.

**c.**

After the first round of this argument, the rabbis who are discussing the *Mishnah* have some questions. When they have questions, they stop and review.

Narrator:  What is the difference between them:

Rabbi Eliezer believes that *Ma'aseh D'ganekha* means "the tithe of your corn" [and not the corn of a non-Jew].

Rabbah believes that *Ma'aseh D'ganekha* should be read as *Ma'aseh D'gnukhah* meaning "the tithe of that which you have [stacked and] stored" [and not that which the non-Jew has stored].

Rabbi Eliezer's point remains constant. He holds that tithes are a *mitzvah*, a Jewish obligation, non-Jews have no such responsibility.

Rabbah's position has now become complicated. Let's unpack it. The assumption behind all these texts is that non-Jewish ownership of property in the Land of Israel should be temporary (really a form of renting, not actual owning). Therefore, at some point, the Jewish owner bears ultimate responsibility. Rabbah's comment on corn assumes that the land has now been "redeemed" (read: repurchased).

Basing his commentary on *Mishnah Ma'aserot* (tithes) 1:6, his explanation of "your storings" is that the Jew is responsible for tithing all corn that has been completed once it has returned to Jewish ownership.

**d.**

At this point, Rabbah steps in and explains his reasoning. He does it using *Mishnah Pe'ah* 4:9, a text we have already studied.

Rabbah:    This is my reasoning:

We have been taught (*Pe'ah* 4:9) that *Leket* (gleanings), *Shikheha* (forgotten sheaves), and *Pe'ah* (produce of the corners) belonging to a non-Jew are still subject to tithing, unless she or he declares them to be public property.

How are we to understand this?

It would be wrong to understand this as teaching that this applies to a field owned by a Jew and harvested by a non-Jew, because then "unless he declares them to be public property" is meaningless because if they were owned by a Jew, these would already be public property.

Therefore, this must refer to a field owned by a

non-Jew, but harvested by a Jew—if he didn't declare them public property, they would still be subject to tithing.

It is here that we understand that part "c" was a tangent, a move away from our solution. While it clearly restates Rabbi Eliezer's central argument, Rabbah's response is not central to his position, but merely a resolution of its meaning. Deuteronomy 14:23 is not central to this argument. Rabbah's consistent view is that non-Jews must tithe land that is under their control. This means that the obligation to tithe should be part of the sales contract a Jew must give when selling property in Israel to a non-Jew (not a law that the government of Israel should come and order them to pay). Rabbah's position is consistently that land in Israel has a continual obligation to be tithed, regardless of ownership.

### e.

Finally, Rabbi Eliezer comes back with a renewed argument. This time, the essence of his concerns comes through as well.

Rabbi Eliezer: [I don't agree. You haven't proven your case.] It is still possible that the field is owned by a Jew, harvested by a non-Jew, and according to your argument was declared public property. Even though *Leket* (gleanings), *Shikheha* (forgotten sheaves), and *Pe'ah* (produce of the corners) are "automatically" considered public property in terms of Jewish perception, are we sure that the non-Jewish harvester will share this perception?

Now we understand that the core of Rabbi Eliezer's concern isn't focused on God's needs; rather it is focused on the *kashrut* of tithing. In essence, he is saying that we can't trust a non-Jew (no matter what the contract) to be responsible for tithing food that a Jew may buy and eat. Therefore, it is the Jewish leaser, the ultimate owner, who must retain the obligation to tithe that land and give its public gifts, regardless of what he or she does with the land (rent or sell with a condition to rebuy before the Jubilee year).

As the *sugiah* (dialogue) continues, a third concern enters into Rabbi Eliezer's argument. It seems that many Jews have sold land to non-Jews and have then failed to redeem it, violating the *mitzvah*. This direct, retained obligation to buy back and bring to the Temple the tithes, etc., extends his or her connection to the land and makes it more likely that it will be redeemed.

In the end, the law follows Rabbi Eliezer. Given that understanding, Rashi, explaining the law, restates the *Mishnah* with which we started.

### *Mishnah*: Rashi's Explanation

If [a Jew] sells his/her field [in the Land of Israel] to a non-Jew, the Jew must still buy the first fruits from the non-Jew each year and bring them to Jerusalem, for the sake of *Tikkun Olam*.

We've learned a number of important insights.

1. The Jews have a unique and special relationship with the Land of Israel that comes with a number of unique responsibilities.

2. Providing God's portion and providing a portion for the poor are Jewish obligations that cannot be sold. I can't sell away my obligation to feed the hungry.

3. Based on the understanding that **"The Land belongs to *Adonai*—also all that fills it,"** *tzedakah* and all the related *mitzvot* of caring directly evolve from the gift of the Promised Land. Later, when these are moved out of the Land of Israel, the same rationale is used, but this time *Aretz* is regeneralized back to "world," making the obligations into obligations that must also be fulfilled outside of the Land of Israel.

## Sunday Will Never Be the Same. . . .

Now we will look at the other side of our equation. We will see how Psalm 24:1 comes to influence our prayer practices. We are going to look at a portion of the talmudic debate on the obligation to say blessings.

Before we begin, here is a little background.

1. The only specific *mitzvah* to say a *brakhah* in the Torah comes in Deuteronomy 6:12: "After you have eaten, and your are satisfied, You should bless *Adonai*, Your God." From this passage, which is really acknowledging the gift of *Eretz Yisrael*, the rabbis generalize the responsibility to give thanks for sustenance.

2. By the time of this passage, lots of other *brakhot* before and after eating are already a common practice. Everyone is already saying *ha-Motzi, Borai P'ri ha-Gafen,* etc. Here, the rabbis question their origins. While they work hard to "prove" that these are *mitzvot* specifically commanded in the Torah, they fail. The best they can do is to make them rabbinic *mitzvot*, something we will do, because it seems to be the right extension of God's stated *mitzvot*.

3. We are now generalizing the principle from just saying a *brakhah* after eating, to saying a *brakhah* as an appreciation of any pleasure.

### Brakhot 35a–b

#### a.

Narrator:   Our rabbis have taught [in a *baraita*]:

Baraita:    It is forbidden for a person to enjoy anything of this world without a *brakhah*. If anyone enjoys anything of this world without a *brakhah*, it is a *ma'al* (sacrilege).

> **Question**: If one has already forgotten [to say the *brakhah*], what is the remedy?
>
> **Answer:** [That person should] consult a wise person?

Rabbi 1:  **Question:** What can a wise person do for him—he has already committed the offense?

Raba:  What it means is that a person should consult a wise person beforehand, so that he can learn the [correct *brakhot*] and not commit a sacrilege.

This piece of *Gemara* reverses everything we've seen in the previous text. Tithing becomes a metaphor, not a legal concern. Here, saying *brakhot* is our focus. The argument is simple. Not saying a *brakhah* before eating (or enjoying) anything that God made is like misusing holy things. The word used in the *baraita* is *ma'al*, a direct reference to Leviticus 5:15, where it says:

> "If a person commits a *ma'al* and sins as a mistake, using that which is Holy to *Adonai* by mistake, then he shall bring as his guilt offering. . . ."

The legal frame here is simple: once something has been dedicated to God (i.e., pledged for a tithe, or an offering, etc.), it belongs to God. It is forbidden for a human to use it or to derive benefit from it. There are, however, conditions under which some of these objects can be "redeemed" and be bought back or replaced. All food that we consume falls into the same category. The *brakhah* is the way we "redeem" the food, taking possession from God. Otherwise, we have literally eaten forbidden fruits.

The second half of this conversation, the one about making atonement, simply suggests that since there is no more Temple, no more sacrifices, no more easy atonement, it is better to get this *brakhah* thing right the first time.

### b.

This second half is a parallel passage. This is not a debate, but a reinforcement.

| | |
|---|---|
| Rav Judah: | Samuel taught, To enjoy anything of this world without a *brakhah* is like making personal use of things consecrated to heaven, since it says [in Psalm 24:1]: |
| Torah: | "The earth is *Adonai's* — also all that fills it. . . ." |
| Rabbi Levi: | [You might think] that a second verse (Psalm 115:16) contradicts this: |
| Torah: | "The heavens are *Adonai's* heavens, but the earth God gave to Adam's children." |
| Rabbi Levi: | But there is no contradiction. The first verse, "The earth is *Adonai's* — also all that fills it . . ." is before the *brakhah* is said, and the second verse, "The heavens are *Adonai's* heavens, but the earth God gave to Adam's children," is after the *brakhah* is said. |

Here, we see some nice verse play. Rabbi Levi parallels the notion that using food (etc.) without a *brakhah* is like taking things that were set aside for holy purposes and using them in a secular fashion. This is then proved, with our verse, Psalm 24:1, "The earth is *Adonai's* — also all that fills it." Rabbi Levi then pulls out the contradictory verse, Psalm 15:23: "The earth God gave to Adam's children." We've seen this juxtaposition of verses before in the previous piece of Talmud. There, Rabbi Eliezer used it to prevent strip mining of the Holy Land (and the like). Here, Rabbi Levi resolves this contradiction in another way. He says that both are true: God owns the world until we say *brakhot*; then God gives it to us *brakhah* by *brakhah*.

c.

Now Rabbi Hanina ben Papa speaks. Here is his sermon.

R. Hanina
b. Papa: To enjoy [anything] in this world without a *brakhah* is like robbing The Holy-One-Who-Is-to-Be-Blessed, and the community of Israel, as it says (in Deuteronomy 32:6):

Torah: "A person who steals from his father or his mother and says, 'It is no crime,' is the companion of a destroyer."

R. Hanina
b. Papa: The **"father"** mentioned here is The Holy-One-Who-Is-to-Be-Blessed, and the **"mother"** mentioned here is the community of Israel. We learn this [from Proverbs 1:8]:

Torah: "Hear, my son, the instruction of your father, and forsake not the teaching of your mother."

**Question**: What is the meaning of "is the companion of a destroyer"?

R. Hanina
b. Papa: He is the companion of Jeroboam son of Nebat, who destroyed Israel's faith in their Father in heaven.

This time the metaphor has been shifted a few degrees. We have moved from *ma'al*, an accidental use of the holy, to "grand theft tomato" or the like. Now eating, smelling, seeking with out a *brakhah* has become a felony charge—metaphorically speaking.

To justify this harsher position, Rabbi Hanina ben Papa plays with a verse from Proverbs. We learn that eating without blessing, (1) violates the Torah's rules, destroying its authority, (2) violates the community of Israel, which is drawn together by the "Our God" part of *Malkhut*, affirming community in every bite, and (3) destroys faith (read: *Ol Malkhut Shamayim*) by secularizing the act of eating, smelling, seeing, etc. Not blessing has become a denial of God The Creator, a refusal to discover God manifested in every creation.

## The Conjunction

The distance from saying a *brakhah* over eating to giving *tzedakah* is not very far. We have taken an elaborate circle to show something that could have been established in a simpler way.

The basic blessing over eating, the one that we met in a *Mishnah* in Chapter 2, is *ha-Motzi*.

הַמּוֹצִיא לֶחֶם מִן הָאָרֶץ
*ha-motzi lehem min ha-aretz*

The One-Who-Brings-Forth bread from the earth.

The "ending" of this *brakhah* is intentionally an enigma. Bread does not grow out of the ground. There are no crescent trees and no bagel bushes—"Bread-Fruit" isn't bread. Bread is a human product. It takes harvesting and threshing and winnowing and grinding and baking and all kinds of things to make wheat or barley or rye into bread. God doesn't directly make bread. A story found in *Midrash Tanhuma, Tazria* 7, makes this point.

Once there was a wicked Roman governor of Judea named Tinneius Rufus. Once he tested Rabbi Akiva by asking him: "Which is more beautiful, the works of God or the works of people.

Rabbi Akiva said, "People's work."

This wasn't the answer the governor was expected. He said sarcastically, "Can a person make heaven and earth?"

Rabbi Akiva answered, "Don't be ridiculous. Don't talk to me about things that are beyond human power. Instead let's compare some of the things that a person can accomplish."

Akiva had ears of corn brought from the field and also beautiful loaves of bread from a bakery. He pointed to the ears of corn and said, "This is the work of God." Then he pointed to the bread and said, "This is human work. Isn't it more beautiful than God's work?"

Next, Akiva had bundles of flax brought in from the field—and also beautifully woven robes. He pointed to the flax and said, "This is God's work." Then he pointed to the robes and said, "This is human work." Then he asked, "Which is more beautiful?"

The point is simple, this *brakhah* over bread, the essential *brakhah* of eating, is not a *brakhah* over wheat—it is an ecosystem *brakhah*—it is recognition of all the differing Divine factors (including people) that go into the production of bread. Bread, the staff of life, is also the quintessential symbol of civilization—the mark of human involvement in completing nature. Bread and its *brakhah* stand as testimony that people complete creation. For Jews, completing creation must include feeding all—that was the reason God provided for all people. Inherent in the act of eating is great responsibility.

## Eight Days a Week: A Retrospective

Our purpose in this section has been to examine the way one single Torah verse expands and grows within the rabbinic tradition. This single verse serves as a model for the way that laws, ceremonies, values, and understandings intertwine and become an organic whole. What we discovered is that the thought pattern that made it a Jewish practice to share between ten and twenty percent of our wealth with those in need shares a common origin with the obligations to bless before and after the consumption of each session of caloric grandizement. Both stem from a single phrase clause: "The earth is *Adonai*'s." That one verse grew a system of tithes, a system of sales rules, a habit of righteousness, a pattern of blessings, and even much more that we haven't begun to uncover. In rabbinic Judaism, every path (read: *halakhah*—law) leads to every other one.

There is no Rome, no single common point, because each ultimately leads to each. One truth begets the next. One insight parents the next. That is the power of association.

It would clearly be overstating the truth to say that the rabbis authored each *brakhah* in such a way that it evoked both a sense of gratitude for God's presence and a sense of obligation for moral action. It would be an overstatement, not because each and every *brakhah* doesn't contain such a duality, but they didn't need to implant it. Given their associative process, and given the cultural background against which the *brakhot* resonate, such pathways are a given.

That's why my friends Rabbi Larry and Rabbi Yosi will never agree. That's why they are both right. That's why I keep both of them around, resonating and echoing in my own ongoing *sugiah* of the mind.

# The Epilogue: A Collation

## The *Brakhah* Formula

This book, about six words—the *brakhah* formula—is about the experiences of God, the process of praying, the history of Jewish thinking, the relationship between Jews and non-Jews, the way to read Torah, the way to read Rashi, the process of *Mishnah*, the patterns of Talmud, and much more. It has been a set of explorations and associations. It is only by rooting oneself in the thought process and cultural setting of the rabbis, in the context the text demands, that word formulae become prayers and that *keva* can evoke *kavanah*. Therefore, we have turned our attention to association, analysis, and exploration, the tools that turn words into prayers, the kinds of prayers that grow and evolve with each repetition.

## Two Metaphors

### Page 89

One of the eternal jokes that makes the rounds every seven or eight years is the story of a group of prisoners who have a joke book. After a while, the book falls apart. Still, they continue to tell the jokes.

Prisoner 1: Page 28 (*All the prisoners laugh*).

Prisoner 2: Page 51 (*All the prisoners laugh*).

Prisoner 3: Page 89 (*We have complete silence*).

Prisoner 1: You always ruin the punch line!

In many ways, the *siddur* is like the oral calling of numbers; it is primarily an act of recalling and reviewing primary Jewish content, not a complete expression of that content.

## The Yearbook

Like everyone else, I keep my old high school year books. Every now and then, when the spirit moves me, I take them out. I flip through, look at pictures, read the signatures, and the like. There is little remarkable about my yearbooks. No one famous signed them. No one famous went to school with me. And, unlike the typical American beer-oriented postfootball hot rod high school fantasy that is so common, high school was not the formative casting of my life's direction. It was just high school: pimples, embarrassment, sexual obsessions, parties, and a lot of red marks and misssspelled [sic] words on a lot of mediocre papers.

Still, every time I open these yearbooks, I feel it. My stomach churns again as some of my major *faux pas* are remembered. I feel some excitement as old infatuations burst from my inner brain, teased by some long hidden memory—and the slides flash in quick succession against some screen behind my retina. Just sitting here in my office, thinking about those four volumes is a powerful moment—right now, I can again smell the locker room. I hated the locker room. It holds no good memories. Still it is there.

When I'm on the road and staying with friends, the guest rooms where I'm placed invariably contain their high school yearbooks, or those of their children. I am an addicted year-book voyeur. Late at night, after everyone is asleep, I open them and look. It is always a disappointment. A few faces are interesting. An occasional line is funny. A rare snapshot contains an interesting image—but essentially they're just a book. Nothing smells. Nothing moves my guts. Nothing reaches within. Each yearbook is an interesting artifact of which Beatle's lyric is placed under which senior photograph, how big the chess team was, and the like—but they don't come alive.

The *siddur* is like a Jewish yearbook. Its word pictures are flat and mechanical to anyone on the outside. If it wasn't your high school, you can appreciate the form, not the substance. But, like the Aladdin High School Yearbook, it waits to be rubbed by memory and association before it shows you the magic.

## The Syntax of Blessing

The *brakhah* formula is six words broken into three parts. On the surface they seem simple enough to form a very obvious statement:

*Adonai*, our God, is blessed.

On the surface there isn't much to say. "God is blessed" is a tautology—a statement of the profoundly obvious. If you believe in God, then obviously "God is blessed." After all, what else does a God do? In a certain sense, it seems that a *brakhah* is simply the affirmation, "I believe in God," which in itself seems redundant, because anyone who is going to go to the effort to say *brakhot* probably believes in God.

Still this little truism, "*Adonai*, our God, is blessed," is designated by the Jewish tradition as something to be said one hundred times a day. It has also been made into the tag line to be fixed to every significant life experience. Having faith in the rabbis' ability to create a vibrant Jewish life leaves only two possibilities. Either it says more than "I believe in God," or there is an important reason for saying "I believe in God" one hundred times a day, and at all of life's significant moments.

Understanding the truth here rests in understanding the meaning of repetition.

When I was in fourth or fifth grade, I learned a joke about a Hispanic man, Jose, who went to his first baseball game, was told that the only available seat was on top of the flag pole, and was honored when everyone in the stadium stood up at the beginning of the game and sang, "Jose can you see?" It reflects a common understanding of our culture, that things endlessly repeated by rote become meaningless. This understanding, while popular, fails to understand the very nature of ritual. When ritual works, it works slowly. It happens over time. Like marathon runners "hitting the wall," "breaking through the pain," and then finding renewed strength, the person who prays continually—the repeat ritualizer—continually breaks through layers of former meaning grown stale and empty, to build new moments of spiritual connection.

In the course of this book we've learned that both possibilities are true. Given the rabbinic process of midrashic association, בָּרוּךְ אַתָּה יהוה אֱלֹהֵינוּ מֶלֶךְ הָעוֹלָם means much more than it says, much more than just "Adonai, our God, is blessed." And, given the nature of the brakhah system's interaction with the mitzvah system, saying "I believe in God" regularly does have the potential to change the universe (if each of those affirmations influences our actions).

## The Barukh

"Brakhah" is both an end and a means, a state-of-being and a process. All this is conveyed in one word: בָּרוּךְ.

Every brakhah begins with בָּרוּךְ. It is a statement that God is barukh, the Source-of-All-Blessings. Each brakhah, however, involves itself only with a small part of the totality of this statement. Each brakhah relates to only one microcosm of God's barukh-ness. A brakhah reflects an instant, a single moment of connection. One brakhah reflects the beauty of a rainbow and the story it recalls. Another expresses the simple joy of recognizing the blessing involved in just eating a piece of bread. A third can respond to basic bodily needs with a renewed awareness that it is a blessing that human body is designed "just right." Each *brakhah* expresses a sense of radical amazement and thanksgiving.

Sometimes a *brakhah* is a reaction, an expression of gratitude for an experience of *brakhah*. We eat, we smell, we see, we hear, we experience some sense of the *brakhot* that the Source-of-All-*Brakhot* has given us—and our response is a *brakhah*, an acknowledgment. At other times, *brakhot* are meditations of preparation. We are about to perform an action: lighting a candle, drinking a cup of wine, eating a piece of bread, etc. In these cases, *brakhot* are the processes that imbue these actions with the possibility of God being present. By saying "thanks" in advance, we prepare ourselves for the possibility of experiencing a *brakhah*.

While the *barukh* in the *brakhah* formula is a statement about God, it is also a statement about us. The side-effect of recognizing God's *barukh*-ness is that it comes with a recognition of our potential to "be a blessing." In this way, *barukh* not only responds to the spiritual by providing us with ways of encountering God, but to the ethical, by inculcating patterns of being like God. In that way, *brakhot* move from actualities to aspirations, from things we experience to things we hope to experience, from ends—the truth about God—to the means that allow us to come close to God by imitating and living up to the Image.

While *barukh* is an adjective, a statement of what God is, it becomes a transitive process, moving from perception to recognition, to aspiration, to imitation, and to actualization. Rub *barukh* with associations and out come Adam, Noah, Abraham, Job, the *Kohanim*, King David, the well, the knees, the gift, the spotlight, the mirror, and more. *Barukh* contains both Rabbi Larry Mahrer and Rabbi Yosi Gordon, the spiritual becoming day-to-day ethics and the business of day-to-day living becoming experiences of God.

Not bad for one word!

## The *Shem*

A classical hasidic story is told about the Maggid of Mezrich. Before he emerged as a world-class rebbe, he started out as a minor-league *heder* teacher. Later, during a hasidic up close and personal, one of his students reported on his teaching style. It went like this: "He used to push us and pull us, ask us questions and listen to us, until each one of us told him our own story of what it was like to go out from Egypt, and until each one of us told him our own story of what it was like to stand at Mount Sinai and receive the Torah." This idea is the extension of an important midrashic concept found in its most popular expression in the *Haggadah*: "Every person is required to see him-/herself as if s/he personally experienced the Exodus from Egypt." In various places, built on various biblical verses, the *midrash* builds a notion that every Jew in every generation was part of the Exodus, part of the revelation at Sinai, part of the teaching of the Holiness Code, and will of course be part of the final redemption. Jewish history becomes a present for every Jew and reliving that past builds the foundations of the Jewish future.

The *Shem* portion, the two Hebrew words, אַתָּה יהוה, embody this concept of constantly relived history.

אַתָּה of course means "You." It addresses God as if God is present, right there before the *brakhah*-sayer. It ignores the formality of addressing the Monarch (as is often the custom) in the third person.

יהוה, as we have discussed at length, is God's private name, a "family" name if you will, that connects God to the experiences of Jewish history.

Together, these two words in the *Shem* portion of the *brakhah* formula conjure up the Jewish experience. Say *Atah Adonai* and it is as if we are directly in God's presence. And, more important, we are there with what the rabbinic tradition calls *zekhut*, "merit." (In modern Hebrew, the slang *protekziah*, holds the same context.) Appearing before God is appearing before The Ruler. However, when we enter this Divine Court, we are entering not as an anonymous subject, but as someone with *zekhut*, with a unique and well-known family background. When we address God as *Atah Adonai*, we are standing in God's presence as the child of Abraham, Sarah, Isaac, Rebekah, Jacob, Leah, Rachel, and all our Jewish ancestors. And, the God we are standing before is the One who called Abram, listened to Sarah laugh, appeared in the Burning Bush, taught Torah to Moses, and much more.

In the moment of saying *Atah Adonai*, we bring all of the Jewish past to our present. It is our way of seeking the future.

## The *Malkhut*

When we address God as אֱלֹהֵינוּ מֶלֶךְ הָעוֹלָם, the *Malkhut* section of the *brakhah* formula, the syntax of address has shifted. As we learned previously, we have shifted from the intimacy of *Atah Adonai* to the more formal address of the Regal Court. *Mahzor Vitry*, which we studied, records the difference as being that between speaking to God "mouth to mouth" and speaking to God "through a messenger."

When we complete the *brakhah* formula, calling God *Eloheinu Melekh ha-Olam*, we are doing more than just giving *Adonai* a compliment—we are doing more than acknowledging God's formal role. Rather, we are taking our stance with the rest of humanity. Not only does the name *Eloheinu Melekh ha-Olam* conjure the universal Creator, the universal Judge, but it simultaneously acknowledges the brotherhood and sisterhood of all humanity. It acknowledges that the future we seek to build with *Adonai* will be the best future for all of humankind. Wonderfully, paradoxically, our most particular secrets have universal aspirations. Saying *Eloheinu Melekh ha-Olam* takes us back from our intimate encounter with the God of our family experience and places us back in a friendship circle with all peoples.

# Putting It All Together

At the beginning of this book we described the *brakhah* formula as the spiritual equivalent of a telephone number, the access code that makes Jewish prayer effective. We reflected on the parts of a telephone number: the long distance indicator, the area code, the prefix, and the specific station number. Each had a role. Each had to come in the right sequence.

Now the time has come to talk about the process of dialing the *brakhah* formula, to see how the parts work together. To do so, we need to point out an unresolved contradiction.

## The Contradiction

In *Midrash ha-Gadol* 12:1, we find the story of how, at age three, Abraham first discovered God. It is the Jewish version of being Davy Crocket. It seems that baby Abram was hidden in a cave, because a wicked king heard a prophecy about the future and wanted to kill all newborn children to protect his throne. (Yes, *midrash* can be a lot like other fantasy literature.) While there, Abram noticed nature at work. At first he thought that the sun was God, because it seemed most powerful and gave life to all. But then a cloud passed in front of the sun and showed its weakness. In succession, Abram believed that the moon, the trees, the stars, etc., were each God—but somehow, as he continued to watch, a greater force emerged. Finally, Abram realized that there must be One Creator God of all things. It was at that moment that God spoke directly to Abram, saying, "I am here, My son."

This piece of *midrash* parallels a lesson we learned in *Mishnah Brakhot* 2:2:

One should first acknowledge *Ol Malkhut Shamayim*
(that *Elohim* is The Ruler-of-the-Cosmos)

and then acknowledge *Ol ha-Mitzvot*
(that *Adonai* revealed the Torah and its *mitzvot* in a covenant with Israel).

That is the exact pattern found in this *midrash*. Abram, the first Jew, first finds God in nature, recognizing what we have called "the God of Aristotle." Then, and only then, Abram receives a revelation, establishing his unique relationship with "the God of Abraham." This pattern of *Malkhut* first, then *mitzvot*, is found in the *Shema* itself, in the *Shema* and its *brakhot*, and the pattern that logic suggests. The *brakhah* formula, of course, rejects the obvious, juxtaposing *zekhut* instead. Unlike Abraham, we have history to guide us and our family's merit to grant us access.

## Dialing the *Brakhah* Formula

The *brakhah* formula defines a process of interacting with the universe. The path it defines is the basic path of all Jewish worship.

Before we utter a word, an opportunity presents itself. It could be an experience we have just had. It could be an experience we are about to have. It could be because we have seen something, or smelled something, or heard something. It could be because the calendar, the clock, and our Jewish awareness have defined a moment as exceptional. It could be because our tradition has required a given action, an action we do regularly, to be more than just a mundane act. Regardless of the stimulus, our Jewish upbringing has conditioned us that a *brakhah* is the correct response. We have been signaled to pay attention, because an encounter with the holy, with the blessing of The Source-of-All-Blessings, is now possible. Even though it is always possible, this particular moment offers an opportunity we know how to actualize. That actualization will come through a *brakhah*.

Like the breath before any utterance, the opportunity begets the words that follow.

The word *barukh* sets the process in motion. It declares the presence of the experience of God. Like throwing a grappling hook, it grabs on to the moment, the stimulus, and declares it an opportunity to encounter God, an opportunity to learn. Simultaneous gratitude and thanksgiving become aspiration and goal.

*Atah Adonai* is a declaration. It is a bold step forward. It is the prideful acknowledgment that the speaker is the rightful heir to a tradition that enables him or her to make meaning of this experience. It says, "Having perceived the holy, I know its Source. In fact, I know the Source's Name. And, more than that, I have studied with the Source's students, know the Source's rules, and have learned how to incorporate this experience into the person I am becoming."

*Eloheinu Melekh ha-Olam* provides balance. It is more than a step back. It is more than an expression of the duality of religious experience. Rather, it is the context. It reminds us that this religious encounter with God is more than a private experience, more than just a moment of personal fulfillment— it is not the end. *Brakhot* aren't about religious ecstasy as a goal; they are a means to redemption. *Eloheinu Melekh ha-Olam* reminds us that there are universal obligations that come with personal privilege.

Then comes the ending, the meat of the *brakhah*. Having prepared, we come to express the uniqueness of the experience that led us to begin the *brakhah*. If nothing else, we have learned that when it comes to *brakhot*, no Jew has the right to remain silent.

# Appendix:
# Primary Sources

Here, freed from the paragraphs that provide one interpretation of them, are the primary texts on which this manuscript is built. Use them for your own study, to expand more than has been provided within this text. Use them to trace your own means and find your own insights. And use them to learn with friends and extend your Torah community.

## Introduction

### I Learned to Pray on the School Yard—
### I Learned to Bless at the Dining Room Table

*Mishnah (Pesahim* **10:6)**

> How [much of the *Hallel*] should one recite [before eating]?:

154

And You Shall Be a Blessing

| The School of Shammai: | Up to [the end of Psalm 113]: "As a joyous mother of children." |
|---|---|
| The School of Hillel: | Up to [the end of Psalm 114:] "The flint into a fountain of water." |
| | Then [the person] "seals" [the recitation with a *brakhah* of] redemption." |
| Rabbi Tarphon: | [Because they did not stipulate a specific *brakhah* formula] for this "seal," we need to indicate one. This *brakhah* should open:] "The One-Who-**Redeemed** Us and **Redeemed** our ancestors from Egpyt." |
| Rabbi Akiva: | [It should close] . . . "Blessed are You, *Adonai*, The One-Who-Has-**Redeemed** Israel." |

### Gemara (Pesahim 117b)

[When the Babylonian rabbis were studying this passage, Raba asked a question about the wording of the closing formula of the *Hallel brakhah*.]

| Raba: | [The last prayer in the] *Shema* [and its *brakhot* (the *Ge'ulah*) and the *brakhah*] after the *Hallel* both end with "The One-Who-Has-**Redeemed** Israel," [which is in the past tense]. |
| | The [fifth *brakhah* in the] *Amidah* [is on the same theme, but it is in the present tense]: The One-Who-**Redeems** Israel. |
| A Voice: | [Why is there a difference?] |

Rabbi
Zera:         The first two are [pure] *brakhot*; the last one is
              a [prayer of] petition.


⊠


# 1    Anything You Say—Can and Will

The *brakhah* formula is made up of four basic elements: the
*Barukh*, the *Shem*, the *Malkhut*, and the *Mitzvah* insertion.

The *brakhah* formula acts as an access code.

### *Brakhot*: A Definition

A *brakhah* is a prayer that uses a formula:

בָּרוּךְ אַתָּה יהוה אֱלֹהֵינוּ מֶלֶךְ הָעוֹלָם
*Barukh Atah Adonai Eloheinu Melekh ha-Olam*

Praised are You *Adonai*, Our God, The Ruler-of-the-Cosmos.

Some *brakhot* insert an additional formula:

אֲשֶׁר קִדְּשָׁנוּ בְּמִצְוֹתָיו וְצִוָּנוּ . . .
*asher kidshanu b'mitzvotav, v'tzivanu . . .*

The One-Who-Makes-Us-Holy with (His) the *mitzvot*, and made
it a *mitzvah* for us. . . .

### The Anatomy of a *Brakhah*

The *brakhah* formula has three distinct parts: The *Barukh*, the
*Shem*, and the *Malkhut*. Each of these parts has a different
function. Each part makes a different spiritual "connection."
(That it is how the formula acts as an access code.)

1. The *Barukh*                                       בָּרוּךְ

Every *brakhah* uses the word *Barukh*. Without it, a prayer is a prayer, not a *brakhah*. *Barukh* is the definitional element in a blessing.

2. The *Shem*                                        אַתָּה יהוה

To be a "kosher" *brakhah* (kosher = acceptable for Jewish use), a *brakhah* must also contain the words: *Atah Adonai*. This portion of the *brakhah* formula is called the *Shem*.

*Shem* means "name." *Adonai* is God's name. (It is like Fred or Barbara.) It is a form of direct address. But it also implies more. It also recalls a specific, intimate relationship. In Chapter 6 of Exodus, God speaks to Moses:

> I am יהוה (*Adonai*).
> I appeared to Abraham, Isaac, and Jacob as *El Shaddai* [God from On High],
> But I did not make Myself known by My Name יהוה *Adonai*
> I also established My covenant with them
> to give them the land of Canaan. . . .

3. *Malkhut*                              אֱלֹהֵינוּ מֶלֶךְ הָעוֹלָם

Every *brakhah* must also contain (or be connected to the phrase *Eloheinu Melekh ha-Olam*. This describes God as *Melekh* (Ruler) and is called *Malkhut*.

*Malkhut* means Rulership. It is a job description. Likewise, *Eloheinu* (Our God) is also a job description. God is a role (fulfilled by *Adonai*).

4. The *Mitzvah* Insertion         . . . אֲשֶׁר קִדְּשָׁנוּ בְּמִצְוֹתָיו וְצִוָּנוּ

⌗

## 2   Preprogrammed Spontaneous Gratification

**The rabbis who wrote our prayers insisted on using a formula because they believed that a "fixed" liturgy is the best path to sincere spiritual "spontaneity."**

## Mishnah (Brakhot 6:1)

### a.

What *brakhot* are said over fruit?

Over the fruit of the tree one says:
בּוֹרֵא פְּרִי הָעֵץ *Borai P'ri ha-Etz*
(The One-Who-Creates the fruit of the tree)

—Except for wine, over which one says:
בּוֹרֵא פְּרִי הַגָּפֶן *Borai P'ri ha-Gafen*
(The One-Who-Creates the fruit of the vine).

### b.

Over things that grow in the ground one says:
בּוֹרֵא פְּרִי הָאֲדָמָה *Borai P'ri ha-Adamah*
(The One-Who-Creates the fruit of the ground)

—Except for bread, over which one says:
הַמּוֹצִיא לֶחֶם מִן הָאָרֶץ *ha-Motzi Lehem min ha-Aretz*
(The One-Who-Brings-Forth bread from the earth).

### c.

Over vegetables one says:
בּוֹרֵא פְּרִי הָאֲדָמָה *Borai P'ri ha-Adamah*
(The One-Who-Creates the fruit of the ground)

—But Rabbi Judah said: One says:
בּוֹרֵא מִינֵי דְשָׁאִים *Borai M'nai De-shaim*
(The One-Who-Creates all kinds of herbs).

## Mishnah (Brakhot 6:2)

If a person says:
בּוֹרֵא פְּרִי הָאֲדָמָה *Borai P'ri ha-Adamah*
(The One-Who-Created the fruit of the ground)
over a fruit that grows on a tree, the *mitzvah* has been fulfilled.

But if one says בּוֹרֵא פְּרִי הָעֵץ *Borai P'ri ha-Etz*
(The One-Who-Created the fruit of the tree)
over fruit that grew in the ground, the *mitzvah* has not been
   fulfilled.

In any case, if the person says
שֶׁהַכֹּל נִהְיֶה בִּדְבָרוֹ *she-ha-Kol Nihiyeh b'Dvar-o*
(That everything was created by His Word),
the *mitzvah* has been fulfilled.

### Gemara (Brakhot 40b)

#### a.

| | |
|---|---|
| Rabbi 1: | [Would it be acceptable for a person to say the *brakhah*: *she-ha-Kol Nehiyeh b'Dvar-o* ("That everything exists because of His Word") over foods that have a specific *brakhah* assigned? |
| Narrator: | [There are two opinions.] We have been taught that Rabbi Huna ruled: |
| Rabbi Huna: | [*she-ha-Kol* is acceptable in every case] except bread and wine. |
| Narrator: | While Rabbi Yohanan ruled: |
| Rabbi Yohanan: | [*she-ha-Kol* is also acceptable] even for bread and wine. |
| [Narrator: | Rashi, a famous medieval Jewish commentator, explains Rabbi Huna's position this way: |
| Rashi: | Bread is an exception, because it is considered to be the essence of a meal. Wine is also a special case because it is connected to *Kiddush*, the perception of holiness. The *Gemara* explains these exceptions later in the discussion on page 42b.] |

## b.

| | |
|---|---|
| Narrator: | [It is clear that even the *Tannaim*, the rabbis of the *Mishnah*] didn't agree about the exact use of *brakhot*. After all,] we have been taught in a *baraita* [a source from the time of the *Mishnah* that was not included in the *Mishnah*, but is quoted here.] |
| Rabbi Meir: | If a person sees a loaf of bread and says: |
| Person: | "What a fine loaf of bread this is! Bless *ha-Makom* [a name for God], Who Created it. |
| Rabbi Meir: | This person has fulfilled the *mitzvah* . . . . |
| Rabbi Yosi: | [I think you are wrong.] If a person changes the formula "minted" by the rabbis, that person has not fulfilled the obligation . . . . |

## c.

To resolve this argument between "form" and "intent," the *Gemara* then cites another old case.

| | |
|---|---|
| Narrator: | [We find Rabbi Meir supported in a famous *baraita* about a ruling Rav made, "The Case of Benjamin's Sandwich."] Benjamin, the shepherd, made a sandwich, [ate it,] and then said in Aramaic [the local language, which is not Hebrew]. |
| Benjamin: | Blessed be The Master-of-this-Bread. |
| Narrator: | [Rav ruled:] |
| Rav: | He has fulfilled his obligation to say a *brakhah* after eating. |

Student:    [No way! That can't be! Wrong! This *brakhah*
            doesn't mention God's name. Anyone could be
            the master of the bread. Benjamin could even
            be blessing himself. How could] Rav [accept
            this as a *brakhah*?] I thought he taught:

Rav:        Any *brakhah* that doesn't mention God's name
            is not a real *brakhah*.

### d.

Narrator:   Then we must guess that [we have remem-
            bered this event incorrectly. We must have
            recalled a wrong version of Benjamin's Ara-
            maic *brakhah*. Because Rav accepted it (and to
            meet his requirement), Benjamin] must have
            said [something like]:

Benjamin:   Blessed be The All-Merciful, The Master-of-
            this-Bread. . . .

### e.

Student:    So what is the point [of this story]? What does
            it teach us [that we don 't already know]? If it
            is to teach us that [it is acceptable] to say a
            *brakhah* in a secular language [and not just
            Hebrew] we have already learned this [lesson].
            It has already been taught [in a *baraita*]:

Baraita:    The following may be said in any language:
            The declaration that a wife has been unfaithful
            [Numbers 5:21], the confession over a tithe
            [Deuteronomy 26:13–15], and the recitation of
            the *Shema*, the *Amidah*, and *Birkat ha-Mazon*.

Narrator:   [While we already knew from this *baraita*] that
            a *brakhah* can be said in any language and not
            just the Holy tongue [the case of Benjamin's

original sandwich *brakhah*] teaches us that even if a person doesn't follow the exact formula "minted" by the rabbis, it can still be acceptable.

### f.

Narrator: Earlier, we mentioned [part of this *baraita*]:

Rav: I think that any *brakhah* that does not mention *Shem* [God's name] is not a real *brakhah*.

Narrator: Rabbi Yohanan disagreed.

Rabbi
Yohanan: Any *brakhah* that doesn't mention [both *Shem* and *Malkhut* (God being the ruler)] isn't a real *brakhah*.

### g.

Abaye: Rav's opinion is probably correct, for it is taught [in Deuteronomy 24:13]:

Torah: "I have not broken any of Your *mitzvot*, and I have not forgotten. . . ,

Abaye: Let me explain:

Torah: "I have not broken any of Your *mitzvot*. . . .

Abaye: means, [I have performed the *mitzvot* of] saying *brakhot* to praise You. . . .

Torah: "and I have not forgotten. . . ."

Abaye: means: "And I have not forgotten to mention *Shem*, Your name. *Malkhut* isn't mentioned [so it is not a requirement. It is nice, but it isn't mandatory].

Narrator:    Rabbi Yohanan understands this verse differ-
             ently. He explains:

Torah:       "And I have not forgotten. . . ."

Yohanan:     means: "I have remembered to mention [both]
             *Shem* and *Malkhut*."

[Rashi:      In the end, the Jewish tradition has followed
             Rabbi Yohanan's position.]

▨

# 3   The Gift That Keeps On Giving

**The function of the *Barukh*—Part 1: From the Bible we learn
that *brakhot* are "gifts" and "aspirations."**

## Numbers 6:22–27

*Adonai* spoke to Moses saying:
Speak to Aaron and to his sons, saying:
This is how you will bless the Families of Israel, saying:

"May *Adonai* bless you and keep you.
May *Adonai* make God's face shine upon you
and be kind to you.
May *Adonai* let God's face turn to you
and give you peace."

And they shall put My name on the Families of Israel,
and I will bless them.

## The Problem

The last sentence, "And they shall put My name on the
Families of Israel, and I will bless them," confused those who
tried to explain this passage. The standard question was, "If

God is doing the blessing, why does God have the priests put the Name on the people?" God shouldn't need a "homing device" to know who to bless (God's *brakhot* should be "smart *brakhot*"—laser targeted).

## Solution 1

In the Talmud, *Hullin* 48a, we find this solution.

"And I will bless them" refers to the sons of Aaron; the *kohanim* (priests) bless Israel and The Holy-One-Who-Is-to-Be-Blessed blesses them.

## Solution 2

In *Midrash Tanhuma*, an early collection of *midrashim*, we find this passage:

The Families of Israel said to The Holy-One-Who-Is-to-Be-Blessed, "The Ruler-of-the-Cosmos, why did you order the *kohanim* to bless us? We need only Your *brakhah*. Please look down from Your Holy habitation and bless Your people.

The Holy-One-Who-Is-to-Be-Blessed answered Israel. Even though I ordered the *kohanim* to bless you, I stand with them and together We bless you.

## Solution 3

Abravanel, the Spanish commentator whose explanation of this verse we have used to organize this passage, takes the hardest line:

*Brakhah* is a homonym (a word with three distinct meanings). It refers to:

a. the **good provided by God** to all God's creatures (as demonstrated by Genesis 24:1, "And *Adonai* blessed Abraham with all. . . . "

b. the **praise directed to God** from people (as demonstrated by I Chronicles 29:10, "And David Blessed *Adonai*. . . . "

c. *brakhot* **given by one person to another**—which should not be confused with the "gifts" provided by God, nor with statements of praise voiced by God's creatures, but rather as a request by the person speaking the blessing, that God provide for the person to be blessed.

## Conclusions

1. For God, *brakhot* are a **commitment**. When God gives a *brakhah*, God insures that this *brakhah* will come true. Because we are created in God's image, striving to live up to that image, our *brakhot* should also be **commitments**.

2. When people say a *brakhah*, it can and should be a **statement of radical appreciation**, an expression of gratitude and praise.

3. When people give a *brakhah*, it can also be a **wish**, a hope that something will become true.

4. If we read the Torah through the eyes of *Midrash Tanhuma*, this very act of "wishing" a *brakhah* may well be **the first step in its actualization**.

⌗

## 4   Imitation Is the Sincerest Form of Blessing

**The function of the *Barukh*—Part 2: From the rabbis we learn that saying *brakhot* is like: jumping in a pool, bowing, and saying "thank you."**

### The Biblical Source: Chapter 12 of Genesis

And I will make you a great nation.
And I will **bless** you.

And I will make your name great.
And you will be a **blessing**.
And I will **bless** those who **bless** you.
(And I will curse anyone who curses you)—
All the families of the earth will be **blessed** through you.

### The Problem

Read this biblical passage and the word *blessing* stands out. So do some questions. "I will bless you" is somewhat obvious. We already have studied the notion that blessings are gifts given by God. Therefore, the following two blessing promises, which make Abraham a source of blessings, seem confusing. "You will be a blessing" is hard to conceptualize as something concrete. So is "All the families of the earth will be blessed through you." The passage stands in need of explanation. How can a person "be" a blessing (especially if God is the source of *brakhah*)? How can all families be blessed through one person?

### *Genesis Rabbah* 39

#### a.

Rabbi Levi said, "No person ever priced a cow belonging to Abraham [in order to buy it] without becoming blessed. No one ever priced a cow [in order to sell it] to Abraham without becoming blessed.

Abraham used to pray for barren women and they were remembered [by God and became pregnant], on behalf of the sick, and they were healed.

#### b.

Rav Huna said, "[That's nothing . . . ] Abraham didn't need to go and actually visit the sick person, [because] once the sick person saw him, he or she was cured."

Rav Hanina said, "[That's nothing . . . ] even ships traveling the sea were saved [through his existence].

### c.

Rav Yitzhak said, "God gave the same kind of *brakhah* to Job. There, [in Chapter 1, verse 10,] it says: 'You [God] have blessed the work of his [Job's] hands.' No one who accepted a penny from Job [in *tzedakah* or in business] ever had to take a second one from him."

### d.

And You Shall Be a Blessing [*Brakhah*]: this means you will be like a *breikhah* [pool]. In the same way that a pool purifies the unclean, so you bring near [to Me] people who are far away.

## Conclusions

a. The foundational understanding of *brakhot* is that they are **gifts** given to people by God. They are promises, about their future, which just by speaking, God makes come true.

b. Likewise, *brakhot* offered by one person to another are essentially **wishes** that God will provide them with *brakhah*.

c. Finally, *brakhot* said by people to God are **acknowledgments** of the gifts that they had received—a liturgical thank you.

d. By making a *brakhah*, it is possible for a person to stand in **partnership** with God, helping to insure the **actualization** of the wish. (This is the explanation given by *Midrash Tanhuma* to the priests' involvement in blessing the people.)

e. The process of living a *brakhah* (making its meaning true), which is, indeed, truly saying it, is a process of **ethical living**—righteousness. (This is the insight found in Rabbi Yitzhak's comparison of Job and Abraham.)

f.  Being a *brakhah* (living out the said words) is a process of finding that part **inside yourself** that connects you to and lets you feel close to God (the teaching of the anonymous *midrash* about the pool).

⊠

# 5    *Adonai* Is a Name, Like "Fred"—God Is a Job Description, Like "A Lawyer"

**The function of the *Shem*—Part 1: The use of God's Name—*Adonai*—is like dialing the family God.**

### Genesis 1:1

Beginnings:
**God** created the heavens and the earth.
The earth was unformed and chaotic.
Darkness was over the deep.
The breath of **God** was over the waters.
**God** said, "Let there be light."
And there was light.
And **God** saw that the light was good.

### Genesis 2:4

This is the family history of the heavens and the earth from their creation.
On the day when the **God**, *Adonai*, made earth and heaven,
there were no bushes and there were no plants growing,
because the **God**, *Adonai*, had not yet made rain.
There was no human to till the soil.
The **God**, *Adonai*, formed Adam from the dust of the soil
and breathed into his nose the breath of life.
Adam came Alive.

### The Problem

Why do the two stories use two different references to God? In other words, why did *Adonai* get added to *Elohim* in the second story?

## Rashi

יהוה (*Adonai*) is God's [actual] name. אֱלֹהִים (*Elohim*) means that God is Ruler and Judge over all. Therefore, whenever the two [God names] appear together, the plain meaning is: "*Adonai*, Who is God (Ruler and Judge)."

## *Genesis Rabbah* 12:15

"*Adonai*, the God, made earth and heaven."

This can be compared to a king who had some empty glasses. Said the king, "If I pour hot water into them, they will burst; if I pour cold water into them, they will contract and snap." So, what did the king do? He mixed hot and cold water and poured it into them, so they remained unbroken.

This is just what The Holy-One-Who-Is-to-Be-Blessed said. "If I create the world on the basis of *mercy* alone, its sins will be great. If I create it on the basis of *justice* alone, the world cannot exist. Hence I will create it on both the basis of judgment and the basis of mercy, and then it may stand!" Therefore, the Torah teaches *Adonai*, the God (*Elohim*).

## *The Kuzari* 4:16

Now I understand the difference between *Adonai* and *Elohim*, and I can see that the God of Abraham is very different from that of Aristotle.

People are drawn to *Adonai* out of love, reason, and conviction, while *Elohim* is compelling as the result of logic.

Religious experiences lead people to give their lives for *Adonai* and to die for *Adonai*'s will. Reasoning, however, makes veneration only a necessity as long as it entails no harm, and as long as no pain results from it.

## *Mahzor Vitry*

The first part of this formula is said as if one were speaking to a King mouth to mouth. Yet in the middle of the *brakhah*, we speak as if to an intermediary.

[Compare "Blessed are You" to please tell the King that . . . "He is Our God, The Ruler-of-the-Cosmos. . . ."]

Now here is the reason. David said (Psalm 16:8): "I have set *Adonai* Before me always . . . ."

[This verse suggests that we can talk directly to God, because *Adonai* is before us.]

In another place (Ezekiel 3:12) the Bible says: "Blessed be the Honor of God from His place."

[This verse teaches that we cannot come close to God, because no one knows where "His Place" is.]

How can we reconcile the two verses? When one is directly addressing God *Barukh Atah Adonai*, it is as David describes; God is before us and we can say "You," speaking with God mouth to mouth. But, when we are blessing God's Honor, *Eloheinu Melekh ha-Olam*, it is as Ezekiel describes, and we must bless God through a messenger.

## Conclusions

As we have stated in the beginning, *Adonai* is the God of Jewish history, The One-Who-Has-Evolved-a-Relationship-to-a-Partic-ular-People through a set of shared experiences and commitments. The Merciful-One, The Torah-Giver, The Purveyor-of-Second-Chances is very much the personal, approachable God—The God-of-Religious Experiences, the God of Abraham.

Likewise, *Elohim*, The Creator, The Absolute Judge, is The One-Who-Is-Accessible-to-All-People through a logical exami-nation of the artifacts of creation. In order words, the order in the creation can reveal the order of The Creator. This is the God Whom the Jewish people share with Aristotle, and all those who seek the truth.

## A Collation

The two God names, *Adonai* and *Elohim*, reflect a series of dualities of religious possibility:

1. *Adonai* = *Elohim*'s Name      *Elohim* = *Adonai*'s role
2. *Adonai* = Mercy      *Elohim* = Justice
3. *Adonai* = The Revealer      *Elohim* = The Creator
4. *Adonai* = God of Jewish history      *Elohim* = Universal God
5. *Adonai* = God of Experience      *Elohim* = God of Logic

# 6     Rumpelstiltskin and Blessing

**The function of the *Shem*—Part 2: The use of God's Name— *Adonai*—is a radical affirmation of the populous grounding of the rabbinic Jewish worship. It empowers everyone.**

## Leviticus 16

"Tell your brother Aaron that he cannot come into the Holy at any time he chooses. He should not go behind 'the Curtain,' which is the cover over the Ark of the Covenant [in the Holy of Holies] for I appear in the cloud over the cover."

Aaron should take the two he-goats and let them stand before *Adonai* at the entrance of the Tent of Meeting. He shall cast lots between the two goats and mark one for *Adonai* and the other for *Azazel*. Aaron shall then take the goat marked for *Adonai* and offer it as a sin offering, while the goat marked for *Azazel* shall be left standing, alive, before the *Adonai*, to make atonement through it, and to send it off to the wilderness for *Azazel*.

At this point, Aaron is to offer his bull as a sin offering for himself and his family. He is to slaughter his bull as a sin offering and then take a panful of glowing coals scooped from the altar before *Adonai*, add two handfuls of finely ground incense, and place this behind "the Curtain" [to the Holy of Holies]. He shall put the incense on the fire before *Adonai*, so that the cloud of smoke from the incense serves as a screen, hiding the Ark of the Covenant, lest he die. . . . When he goes in to make atonement in the Tabernacle, nobody else shall be in the Tent of Meeting until he comes out. . . .

When he has finished purging the Tabernacle, the Tent of Meeting, and the altar, the live goat is brought forward. Aaron shall lay both his hands upon the head of the live goat and confess over it all the missed marks and transgressions of the Families of Israel, putting them on the head of the goat, and it shall be sent off to the wilderness . . . thus the goat shall carry on him all their sins to an inaccessible region. . . .

### Mishnah (Yoma 6:2)

Next he came to the Scapegoat and placed his two hands [between the horns] and confessed. This is what he said:

"I pray, **The Name**

Your People, the House of Israel, have done wrong, they have missed-the-mark, they have transgressed before You.

I pray [with] **The Name**

Please forgive the iniquities, the transgressions, and the missed-marks that Your People, the House of Israel have erred before You."

As it is written in the Torah of Moses, Your servant (Leviticus 16:30): "For on this day will atonement be made for you, to make you clean from all your missed-marks. Before יהוה you shall become clean."

And when the *Kohanim* who were standing in the courtyard heard יהוה, "**The Unspoken Name**," pronounced from the *Kohein* *ha-Gadol*'s mouth, they went down, knelt, fell on their faces, and said:

בָּרוּךְ שֵׁם כְּבוֹד מַלְכוּתוֹ לְעוֹלָם וָעֶד

*Barukh Shem Kevod Malkhuto le-Olam va-Ed*

*Barukh* be **the Name** Whose Honored Kingdom is for eternity and more.

### Kiddushin 71a

**a.**

| | |
|---|---|
| Rabbah ben Bar Hanah: | Rabbi Yohanan said: |
| Rabbi Yohanan: | The sages only taught the pronunciation of the Tetragrammaton to their disciples once in a cycle of seven. |
| Narrator: | Others say they taught its pronunciation twice a cycle of seven. |
| Rabbi Nahman ben Isaac: | Logic suggests that it was [no more often] than once in a cycle of seven because it says [in Exodus 3:15]: |
| Torah: | זֶה־שְּׁמִי לְעֹלָם<br>This is My Eternal Name [*le-Olam*]. |
| Rabbi Nahman ben Isaac: | [But] in the Torah, [the word] לְעוֹלָם is written [without the letter ו, making it] לְעַלֵּם [which means "to be kept secret]." |

Raba was once planning to give a public lecture on this topic, but a certain old man said to him:

Old Man: It is written in the Torah: לְעֹלָם—to be kept secret.

Rabbi
Nahman
ben Isaac: Raba then canceled the lecture.

## b.

Narrator: Rabbi Abina [taught a lesson] by connecting the two [parts of that] verse:

Rabbi
Abina: [In Exodus 3:15] God says:

Torah: This is my name:

Rabbi
Abina: [And later in that verse God says]:

Torah: This is My Memorial.

Rabbi
Abina: The Holy-One-Who-Is-to-Be-Blessed [put these two phrases together] to say, "I am not to be called (memorialized) the same way I am written (My Name). My name is to be written יה, but it is to be pronounced *Adonai*.

## c.

Narrator: Our rabbis taught:

*Baraita*: At first all of the people [of Israel] were trusted with the twelve-letter Name [of God]. Then, when many of them grew to be unfit, its [knowledge] was limited to the pious *kohanim*, and they [made it a practice] to swallow its [pronunciation] when they said it [during the priestly benediction] with their brother priests.

Narrator:   It is taught:

Rabbi
Tarfon:     I once went up on the *bimah*, following my
            mother's brothers, and listened carefully to the
            *Kohein ha-Gadol*. I actually heard him swallow
            the Name during the chanting of his brother
            priests.

### d.

Rabbi
Judah:      Rav taught:

Rav:        The forty-two-letter name of God is only en-
            trusted to a person who is pious, meek, middle-
            aged, free from bad temper, sober, not insis-
            tent on his rights. One who knows this name is
            careful of it and observes its purity, is popular
            above and popular below, is held in awe by
            people, and inherits two worlds: this world
            and the world to come.

## 7  Desired Ambivalence

The function of the *Malkhut*: The God descripter, *Elohim*,
defines God as a Judge. Its use in the *Malkhut* section,
connects the Creater-of-the-Cosmos to the creation of
universal ethics. Each of the names we call God (*Shem* and
*Malkhut*) not only defines an aspect of God (or an aspect of
our relationship with God) but also a set of obligations. The
use of *Adonai* involves us in *Ol ha-Mitzvot* (The "Yoke" of
the *Mitzvot*), while the use of *Elohim* involves us in *Ol
Malkhut Shamayim* (The "Yoke" of God's Cosmic
Rulership).

### Sanhedrin 59a

Rabbi
Yohanan:    A non-Jew who studies the Torah deserves to
            die, for it is taught [in Deuteronomy 33:4]:

Torah:      "Moses commanded us Torah as an inherit-
            ance."

Rabbi
Yohanan:    [Torah] is our inheritance, not theirs. [By
            studying it, is like stealing it from us. For that
            they deserve death.]

A Rabbi:    Then why wasn't this prohibition also included
            in the seven *mitzvot* given to Noah?

Rabbi
Meir:       We've been taught, "A non-Jew who studies
            the Torah is as holy as the *Kohein ha-Gadol*. It
            comes from [Leviticus 8:5]:

Torah:      "You shall therefore keep My statutes and My
            judgments, by following these, a **person** shall
            **live**.

Rabbi
Meir:       [The Torah] doesn't say "a priest," it doesn't
            say "a Levite," it doesn't even say "an Israel-
            ite"—it just says "a **person**"—therefore "any
            person" who studies Torah is equal to the
            *Kohein ha-Gadol*.

Rabbi:      I think that non-Jews should be limited to
            portions that involve the seven *mitzvot* of Noah
            [the laws they are responsible to enact].

### *Exodus Rabbah* 30:9

Another explanation of:
**"Now these are the judgments"**

#### a.

It is written in Psalm 147:19–20:
**"He tells his דְּבָר [word] to Jacob."**
*Davar* [word] means the Ten Commandments (עֲשֶׂרֶת הַדִּבְּרוֹת,
*Asseret ha-Dibrot*).

"חֻקָּיו [His statutes] וּמִשְׁפָּטָיו [And His judgments] to Israel."
This means His judgments.

## b.

God does things differently from people.
One person will order another,
to do something that he, himself, will not do.
But God only tells Israel to do and observe those things
which God (Himself) also does.

## c.

A story about Rabban Gamliel, Rabbi Joshua, Rabbi Eliezer
    ben Azaria, and Rabbi Akiva.
They went to Rome and taught there:
"God does things differently than people do.
People enjoy ordering others around while doing nothing
    themselves—
God doesn't work that way."

An apostate Jew was listening to them,
and heckled them as they were leaving with this question:
"Didn't you just say that God says a thing and fulfills it.
[If that is the case] why doesn't God observe the Shabbat
    prohibitions?
[After all, doesn't God cause the wind to carry things
from one place to another on Shabbat.]
"Fool!" they answered him, "Isn't a person permitted to carry
    things within his own courtyard on Shabbat?
He answered, "Yes."
Then they told him, "Both the upper and lower regions are
    the courtyard of God. We learn this from [Isaiah 6:3]:
'The whole earth is full of His Glory. . . .'"

## d.

Another explanation of:
**"He tells his word to Jacob."**
Rabbi Abbahu taught in the name of Rabbi Yose b. Hanina:
This can be compared to a king who had an orchard.

In it he planted all kinds of trees.
He was the only one who entered this garden—
he, himself, was its keeper.
When his children came of age, he said to them:
"My children,
up to now I guarded this garden.
I didn't allow anyone else to enter it.
Now, I want you to keep this garden as I have."

### e.

This is what God [the King] said to Israel [His Children]:
"Prior to My creation of the cosmos, I prepared the Torah,
that is the meaning of Proverbs 8:30:
**'I was with Him as an אָמוֹן amon [nursling]'**—this means 'a
tutor.'
'It is explained by comparison with Numbers 11:12:
**'As an אֹמֵן oman [nursing father] carries a sucking child.'**
I did not give the Torah to heathens,
rather I gave to Israel as soon as they said (Exodus 24:7):
**'All Adonai has Spoken, we will do and we will obey.'"**

This is the meaning of:
**"He tells his word to Jacob,**
His statutes And His judgments to Israel."

**"He didn't do this for any of the other Nations**
His judgments they have not known.
Hallelujah."

Only Jacob, whom God chose from all the heathen peoples,
received the whole Torah [all 613 commandments].
God gave Adam six commandments.
God added one for Noah.
Abraham had eight.
And Jacob had nine.
But to Israel, God gave them all.

### f.

Rabbi Simon said in the name of Rabbi Hanina:
"It can be compared to a king who sat at a banquet table

set with all kinds of dishes.
When his first servant entered, he gave him a slice of meat.
When the second entered, he gave him an egg.
When the third entered, he gave some vegetables.
He gave a portion to each one separately.
When his son came in, he gave him all that was before him, saying to him:
'To the others I gave only a single portion, but to you I give all.'

"So also God gave the heathen only some odd commandments,
but when Israel arose, God said to them:
'Behold, the whole Torah is yours.'
This is the meaning of:
**'He didn't do this for any of the other Nations.' "**

## g.

Rabbi Eleazer said:
"It can be compared to a king who went out to war with his troops.
When he slaughtered an animal, he would distribute each piece proportionally [according to the number in each division].
His son was watching this distribution and asked:
'What [portion] will you give to me?'
The king answered:
'[I will give you] from that which I have prepared myself.'
So God gave to the heathens, commandments as it were, in their raw state,
for them to toil over [and actualize],
not making any distinction between uncleanness and purity;
but as Israel came,
God explained each precept separately to them—
the punishment [for not fulfilling it] and its reward.
This is the meaning of Song of Songs 1:2,
**'Let him kiss me with the kisses of his mouth.'**

"This is the meaning of:
**'His statutes and His judgments [God Taught] to Israel.' "**

## A Review:

1. The *Malkhut* section involves (a) using God's name *Elohim* (the job description) and (b) mentioning that God is *Melekh ha-Olam* (The Ruler-of-the-Cosmos).

2. The name *Elohim* implies three things, (a) that God is a Judge (*Midat ha-Din*); (b) that God is the Universal Creator (transcendent); and (c) that God is accessible to all people (what Yehuda ha-Levi calls "the God of Aristotle").

3. The *Malkhut* section is connected to the acceptance of God as The Ruler-of-the-Cosmos (*Ol Malkhut Shamayim*).

4. God's revelation of Justice came in two basic thrusts, seven *mitzvot* to Noah's children (all of humanity) and 613 *mitzvot* (the whole Torah) to the Jewish people.

# 8 Eating the Ethical

**Saying a *brakhah* impacts upon us two ways: spiritually and ethically. It is like shining a spot light and focusing our gratitude. It is like looking in a mirror and adjusting the way we are living up to God's image.**

### The *Midrash* on Psalm 24:3 (A Fragment)

The Holy-One-Who-Is-to-Be-Blessed:
Created the days [of the week] and took *Shabbat* as God's portion,
Created the moon-cycles and chose the festivals as God's portion,
Created the years and chose the sabbatical year as God's portion,
Created the nations [of the world] and chose Israel as God's portion. . . .

Created the lands [of the earth] and took as God's portion
The Land of Israel as a heave-offering from all the other
   lands:

This is learned from Psalm 24:1
**"The Land belongs to *Adonai*—also all that fills it."**

## *Exodus Rabbah* 41:1 (A Fragment)

Rabbi Nehemiah said:
. . . Ordinarily, when one gives a field over to a tenant,
the tenant must supply both the seeds and the labor,
and still the owner receives fifty percent of the produce.
Yet, The Holy-One-Who-Is-to-Be-Blessed—
God's Name is to be praised, God's mention is to be extolled
doesn't work that way.

We are taught in Psalm 24:1:
**"The Land belongs to Adonai—also all that fills it."**
Both the Land and its seeds belong to God,
He also causes the rains to fall,
the dews to spring forth—
these [work] to make the fruit grow, and remain fresh.
God does all kinds of work to grow fruit.
Yet God says to Israel:
"I have only commanded you to give me one-tenth . . . as My
   portion."

## *Pe'ah* 4:9

A person who collected the *Pe'ah* [from his field and] said:
"This I have set aside for a specific poor person"—

Rabbi Eliezer says:
"That person has given ownership of that produce to that
   particular poor person."

The sages say:
"[Wrong!] The [owner] must give it to the first poor person
   whom [s/he] meets first."

*Leket, Shikheha,* and *Pe'ah* that belong to a non-Jew must be
   tithed, unless s/he declares them to be public property.

## Gittin 47a

### Mishnah

If a Jew sells his/her field [in the Land of Israel] to a non-Jew,
the one who purchased it
must still take and bring from it the first fruits,
for the sake of *Tikkun Olam*.

### Gemara

#### a.

Rabbah:   Even though a non-Jew can purchase property
          in the Land of Israel, [his or her ownership is
          not to be complete—even though he or she is
          not Jewish and therefore subject to Jewish law,
          the conditions of sale to him/her] must not
          release the property from the [*mitzvah* of] tith-
          ing, since it says in Leviticus 25:23-24:

Torah:    "The Land must not be sold beyond reclaim,
          For the Land is Mine.
          You are only Foreigners Dwelling with Me.
          In all the Land that You hold,
          you must provide for the Redemption of the
          Land."

Rabbah:   "The Land is Mine" essentially says: Its holi-
          ness [meaning its tithes,] are Mine, [sales to a
          non-Jew must not mitigate the obligation to
          tithe].

          However, a property sale to a non-Jew may
          give him/her the right to dig pits, ditches,
          caves, etc. We learn this from the Psalm 15:16:

Bible:    "The heavens are *Adonai*'s heavens.
          The earth is given to Adam's children."

b.

Rabbi
Eliezer:    [I disagree.] A non-Jew can [be allowed to]
            own property in the Land of Israel [without
            retaining the] obligation to tithe. This can be
            learned from Deuteronomy 14:22–23:

Torah:      "Each year you should set aside one-tenth of
            the crop. You should eat these tithes before
            *Adonai*, your God, in the place where God will
            choose to establish His Name,
            מַעְשַׂר דְּגָנֶךָ
            *Ma'aseh D'ganekha*
            the tithe of your corn,
            the tithe of your wine, the tithe of your oil, the
            tithe of your firstborn animals, the tithe of your
            flocks—so that you will learn to be in Awe of
            *Adonai*, your God."

Rabbi
Eliezer:    The Torah teaches: "The tithe of your corn,"
            which implies [your corn and] not the corn of
            non-Jews.

            However, a non-Jew [should not be sold prop-
            erty in the Land of Israel under conditions that
            allow him or her] to dig pits, ditches, or caves.
            We learn this from Psalm 24:1:

Bible:      "The Earth belongs to *Adonai*. . . ."

c.

Narrator:   What is the difference between them:

            Rabbi Eliezer believes that *Ma'aseh D'ganekha*
            means "the tithe of your corn" [and not the
            corn of a non-Jew].

Rabbah believes that *Ma'aseh D'ganekha* should be read as *Ma'aseh D'gunekhah* meaning "the tithe of that which you have [stacked and] stored" [and not that which the non-Jew has stored].

Rabbah:    This is my reasoning:

We have been taught (*Pe'ah* 4:9) that *Leket* (gleanings), *Shikheha* (forgotten sheaves), and *Pe'ah* (produce of the corners) belonging to a non-Jew are still subject to tithing, unless she or he declares them to be public property.

How are we to understand this?

It would be wrong to understand this as teaching that this applies to a field owned by a Jew and harvested by a non-Jew, because then "unless he declares them to be public property" is meaningless because if they were owned by a Jew, these would already be public property.

Therefore, this must refer to a field owned by a non-Jew, but harvested by a Jew—if he didn't declare them public property, they would still be subject to tithing.

e.

Rabbi
Eliezer:    [I don't agree. You haven't proven your case.] It is still possible that the field is owned by a Jew, harvested by a non-Jew, and according to your argument was declared public property. Even though *Leket* (gleanings), *Shikheha* (forgotten sheaves), and *Pe'ah* (produce of the corners) are "automatically" considered public

property in terms of Jewish perception, are we sure that the non-Jewish harvester will share this perception?

### *Mishnah*: Rashi's Explanation

If [a Jew] sells his/her field [in the Land of Israel] to a non-Jew, the Jew must still buy the first fruits from the non-Jew each year and bring them to Jerusalem, for the sake of *Tikkun Olam*.

## Conclusions

1. The Jews have a unique and special relationship with the Land of Israel that comes with a number of unique responsibilities.

2. Providing God's portion and providing a portion for the poor are Jewish obligations that cannot be sold. I can't sell away my obligation to feed the hungry.

3. Based on the understanding that **"The Land belongs to Adonai—also all that fills it,"** *tzedakah* and all the related *mitzvot* of caring directly evolve from the gift of the Promised Land. Later, when these are moved out of the Land of Israel, the same rationale is used, but this time *Aretz* is regeneralized back to "world," making the obligations into obligations that must also be fulfilled outside of the Land of Israel.

### *Brakhot* 35a–b

#### a.

Narrator:   Our rabbis have taught [in a *baraita*]:

Baraita:    It is forbidden for a person to enjoy anything of this world without a *brakhah*. If anyone enjoys anything of this world without a *brakhah*, it is a *ma'al* (sacrilege).

> **Question**: If one has already forgotten [to say the *brakhah*], what is the remedy?
>
> **Answer**: [That person should] consult a wise person?

Rabbi 1: **Question**: What can a wise person do for him— he has already committed the offense?

Raba: What it means is that a person should consult a wise person beforehand, so that he can learn the [correct *brakhot*] and not commit a sacrilege.

### b.

Rav
Judah: Samuel taught, To enjoy anything of this world without a *brakhah* is like making personal use of things consecrated to heaven, since it says [in Psalm 24:1]:

Torah: "The earth is *Adonai*'s—also all that fills it . . . ."

Rabbi
Levi: [You might think] that a second verse (Psalm 115:16) contradicts this:

Torah: "The heavens are *Adonai*'s heavens, but the earth God gave to Adam's children."

Rabbi
Levi: But there is no contradiction. The first verse, "The earth is *Adonai*'s—also all that fills it . . ." is before the *brakhah* is said, and the second verse, "The heavens are *Adonai*'s heavens, But the earth God gave to Adam's children," is after the *brakhah* is said.

### c.

Now Rabbi Hanina ben Papa speaks. Here is his sermon.

R. Hanina
b. Papa:    To enjoy [anything] in this world without a
            *brakhah* is like robbing The Holy-One-Who-
            Is-to-Be-Blessed, and the community of Israel,
            as it says (in Deuteronomy 32:6):

Torah:      "A person who steals from his father or his
            mother and says, 'It is no crime,' is the com-
            panion of a destroyer."

R. Hanina
b. Papa:    The "**father**" mentioned here is The Holy-One-
            Who-Is-to-Be-Blessed, and the "**mother**" men-
            tioned here is the community of Israel. We
            learn this [from Proverbs 1:8]:

Torah:      "Hear, my son, the instruction of your father,
            and forsake not the teaching of your mother."

            **Question**: What is the meaning of "is the
            companion of a destroyer"?

R. Hanina
b. Papa:    He is the companion of Jeroboam son of Nebat,
            who destroyed Israel's faith in their Father in
            heaven.

# Index

187